LET ME TELL YOU A STORY

Let Me Tell You A Story

TIM WAGGONER

GUIDE DOG BOOKS

RAW DOG SCREAMING PRESS

www.RawDogScreaming.com

Cover Design © 2023 by C.V. Hunt

Interior Layout by D. Harlan Wilson
www.dharlanwilson.com

Guide Dog Books
Bowie, MD

TABLE OF CONTENTS

Foreword • 7

Huntress • 11

Alacrity's Spectatorium • 34

Mr. Punch • 47

Daddy • 62

Keeping It Together • 67

Ghost in the Graveyard • 85

Joyless Forms • 96

Broken Glass and Gasoline • 103

Waters Dark and Deep • 124

Swimming Lessons • 147

Long Way Home • 152

Sharp as Night • 181

Til Death • 191

How to be a Horror Writer • 211

Afterword • 224

Acknowledgements • 225

FOREWORD
ARE YOU KIDDING ME?
ANOTHER DAMN WRITING BOOK?

After *Writing in the Dark,* I swore I'd never do another how-to-write book. Once I finished it, I thought I'd said all I had to say about writing fiction in general and horror in particular. Sure, as the years passed and my knowledge (hopefully) increased, I might feel inspired to do another how-to, but for now, I figured my blog posts and newsletter articles about writing would be more than enough.

Then I wrote *Writing in the Dark: The Workbook.*

One of the things readers liked most about the first volume was the exercises that appeared at the end of each chapter. That got me thinking ... Could I write an entire book of horror-writing exercises? I wasn't certain, but it sounded like a fun challenge—and obviously there were readers who'd like to have such a book—so I decided to give it a go. *Writing in the Dark* poured out of me like water when I wrote it, and I was surprised to find that the workbook did so too. But when I finished the workbook, I vowed that I wouldn't write another follow-up—at least for a while—and I fully intended to stick by this.

I've been writing about writing for decades. In my late teens, I began reading *Writers' Digest* religiously, and my favorite part of the magazine was Lawrence Block's monthly column on writing fiction. (This is why I dedicated *Writing in the Dark* to him.) I became fascinated by the art of writing about writing, and after I began selling fiction and articles professionally, I decided to give it a go. I published a number of how-to-write articles over the years, and when I started a blog over a decade ago, I decided I'd use it as an outlet for writing about writing.

Still, I wanted to do my own how-to-write book, so I wrote various proposals and gave them to my agent to send around, but no publishers were interested. Then I came up with the idea of writing a *horror* how-to, and John and Jennifer loved the idea, and the rest is history. I told my agent to forget about the previous how-to-write proposals I'd sent her, and I went back to writing fiction full-time. A couple years passed, and my agent— who hadn't deleted my old proposals—remembered one for a book called *Let Me Tell You a Story*. I'd originally intended it to be an overall volume on writing fiction, but I'd incorporated so much of that kind of material in *Writing in the Dark*, I abandoned the idea of writing a generic how-to. My agent sent the proposal to Jennifer, who liked it, and offered a contract—for a book I had no intention of writing.

I've been writing professionally for too long to immediately turn down a publisher's offer without at least thinking about it. And my previous two experiences working with Jennifer and John were wonderful, so I was excited by the prospect of working with them again. But what the hell would this new book be about? I knew I couldn't write the generic how-to-write book I'd originally envisioned for *Let Me Tell You a Story*, but there was nothing about the title that suggested a way to turn it into a third volume on writing horror. I decided I'd figure something out eventually, so I signed the contract.

Days, weeks, months passed. I worked on other projects, but I kept thinking about *Let Me Tell You Story* and wrestling with what the book should be. More time passed. The deadline for turning in the manuscript approached, and I still had nothing. This was very unlike me. Usually when I've contracted to do a book, I finish it early. Not this time. I told Jennifer, and she kindly understood and gave me an extension, but I was afraid I'd never figure out a way to move forward with *Let Me Tell You a Story*. If I couldn't, I'd have to back out of the contract, which was something I'd never done before. But, as so often happens in my writing life, when I thought all was lost, an idea popped into my head.

I'd written *Writing in the Dark: The Workbook* solely because of reader feedback I'd received on the first volume. Was there anything else readers liked about the first two books that might serve as inspiration for a third volume? Yes, there was. In each of the previous books, I included a short story of mine and critiqued it based on the principles outlined in the books. I talked about what worked, what didn't, and what I might do differently if I had the chance to rewrite the story.

What if I focused an entire book on examining a collection of my stories, discussing their origins, my intentions for them, how well they'd worked, and what—if anything—I'd change now. Such a book would be an odd duck, part short story collection, part how-to-write, part memoir, and part career retrospective. The idea of working with a hybrid format like this appealed to me. And it wasn't as if I hadn't encountered similar books before. One of my favorites is science fiction writer Mike Resnick's *Putting It Together: Turning Sow's Ear Drafts into Silk Purse Stories*. In it, Mike presents several of his stories and shows how they went from idea to multiple drafts to finished version. The idea behind his approach was that any how-to-write book can *tell* you how to create developed characters, write engaging dialogue, etc., but by detailing his writing process, he could *show* you how to do it, or at least how he did it. And of course, Stephen King's *On Writing* is a blend of how-to and memoir.

As I contemplated this new approach for *Let Me Tell You a Story*, I had some concerns. What if readers viewed the book as one long ego trip on my part? *Check out all these fabulous stories! Aren't I a great writer?* What if readers didn't give a damn about my fiction and only wanted how-to-write advice? What if, by being neither fish nor fowl—not fully a writing instruction guide or a short story collection—the book failed to find an audience? I've always enjoyed reading authors' story notes in collections, though, and I feel I learn more when authors share specifics about how they create their work as opposed to offering generic advice, so I figured, what the hell? Why not go for it?

So I did.

How did I choose the stories included in this book? I decided to include stories that were pivotal in my development as a writer, stories where I learned important lessons or made mistakes that I only recognized in hindsight. I've arranged the stories in chronological order because that seemed simplest, and because that will hopefully create a portrait of my development as a writer as well.

In terms of the type of stories I've included, while I've written in different genres, I'm known primarily as a horror/dark fantasy author, so I stuck to those genres rather than put in a fantasy or science fiction story here and there. It seemed to make more thematic sense to me.

And after each story, I've included commentary/reflection, as well as a couple writing exercises so you can take the focus off my work and put it on yours, where it belongs.

You're welcome to read and use this book however you wish, as a writing instruction guide, as a short story collection, or as an inside look at how one writer created his stories and what he thinks about them today. It's as much a portrait of an artist as it is a how-to, and I hope whatever you came here for, you find the book both enjoyable and useful.

So let's get started.

HUNTRESS

Originally published in *Tamaqua* (Winter/Spring 1990)
Reprinted in *The Mythic Circle* (Fall 1993)

This was my first time at Basin Street. I make it a rule never to visit the same place twice. Not that I fear detection or capture. If I were detected it would yield little more than a headline on a cheap supermarket tabloid. And capture is a distinct impossibility. You can't hold a spirit. Not when it doesn't wish to be held.

I was more than a spirit that night. My form was that of a woman, mid-twenties, with brunette hair which hung in bangs over my forehead and touched the back of my neck. My skin was pale, my lips red. I wore a white blouse and blue jeans. My body was long and thin—a model's body. Not the pipe cleaner-limbed languidness of Europe, but rather the controlled sexuality of, if not the girl next door, the woman in the next office. The one who sells business suits by managing to make them look like teddies. It was one of my most effective guises. I thought it would work well for this night.

I was waiting alone at a table just big enough for two. The wait used to be my favorite part of the hunt, back when it was all new to me, but that was centuries ago. At first it was exciting, delirious. I walked like a god among mortals. Now, after thousands, hundreds of thousands of nights like this one, I no longer felt like a god. I saw myself, on those few occasions that I even bothered to think about it, as a shark. And like a shark, which must swim constantly in order to extract oxygen from the water, I traveled without let.

One night a bar, another a street corner, another a back alley ...
And I gave as much thought to these places as a shark did to the
water it swims in. Now the waiting wasn't anything to me.

Dance music throbbed from gigantic speakers, a driving
beat overlayed with electronic runs that were supposed to
sound like bells. The music filled the room with a constant
beat I could feel through the floor. I prefer to sit right next
to a speaker and let the music fill me, but it discourages conversation, so I don't usually indulge myself. At the table next
to me sat a ram-headed man dressed in a green robe. He was
drinking beer through a straw and talking with a girl whose
tight red leotard sported a forked tail. A horned tiara topped
off her ensemble. Her companion's mask was amateurish. The
hair was obviously fake and the horns were far too short to be
menacing. Still, it was amusing.

A woman in a black dress, low cut and torn at the hem, with
red nails and raven circles around her eyes walked past, her arms
around the waist of a young man in a gargoyle mask wearing a
T-shirt which read "Go to Hell." I smiled as they went by and lit
a cigarette.

The bar was tended by a pair of men with bloody homemade
scars on their faces, necks, arms—it seemed every bit of their
exposed flesh was covered by lipstick-red welts. They had wrapped
themselves in chains. I supposed them to be the Damned, though
they were far too cheerful to be convincing.

I wondered what these costumed children would think could
they meet the cold, harsh shadows they mocked. Shadows such
as myself. The thought turned my smile into a grin.

A waitress came by and I ordered a glass of burgundy. As I
waited for my drink, I watched the dance floor. It was filled with
all manner of creatures jumping and swaying to the music. As I
watched, a man who couldn't have been more than twenty-five
approached me. He was wearing a charcoal gray business suit.
His hair was slicked back and he wore a false goatee. It was time
for it to begin and I realized with a bit of a shock that I was
disappointed. In the back of my mind I was already wondering
where I would be tomorrow night.

"Good evening, my dear," he said cheerfully. He thrust paper and pen at me. "Would you be interested in the deal of a lifetime?"

I took his pen and laughed. He stood patiently, a smile on his lips. I glanced over his contract. He'd done it in red ink, to resemble blood. He'd even gone to the trouble to smear it in a few places. The irony was delicious.

"Where do I sign?"

He smiled back. "At the bottom, of course." He spoke loudly to be heard over the music, but in an easy manner. Still, I could feel his nervousness. He was uncertain of himself, yet he was here. I liked that.

"Would you like to sit down so we can discuss terms?"

For a moment I thought I had been too direct. He hesitated, and I thought he would mumble some excuse and go, but then he smiled again and sat down.

"I think you'll find my terms very reasonable."

"I'm sure I will." The waitress brought me my drink. He insisted on paying for it and ordered himself a Michelob. I thanked him politely, then sipped my wine, waiting for him to make a move.

"My name's Jerry."

"Mine's Lana."

"Pleased to meet you, Lana." He offered his hand. I found it a most endearing gesture. I held his hand for just a half-second too long. I tasted his flesh through mine, drank in the salty-sweetness of his skin.

The waitress returned with his beer. He took a long sip, his eyes scanning the dancers. I knew from experience he was buying time to think of what he would say next. I took the opportunity to examine him more closely. His hair was more brown than black. It would be much lighter whenever he washed out the substance he'd used to slick it back. His face was thin. It was a face that hovered on the edge of appearing unhealthy. But that didn't bother me. Bodies are merely empty shells. It's what fills them that is important. I caught his light-green eyes and in the instant I held his gaze, I bored into and down to his soul. Most people's souls are hidden, buried deep within the flesh, but his was close to the surface. It was one of the purest I'd seen in a very long time. My need screamed at me to take him right then. But I restrained myself. There would be time for that later.

The contract lay on the table between us. He rolled it up carefully and replaced it inside his jacket, slipping it into a pocket behind a small pad of drawing paper.

I smiled gently. "Are you an artist?"

He opened his mouth to deny it, then sighed. "Not really. I play around with it some, but that's about it."

I understood now why the contract had been so well done. He had a talent for this sort of thing. "Is that a sketch pad? I'd like to see it."

He looked embarrassed. "I'd really rather not."

"Please?"

He was uncomfortable, but he gave in and handed me the pad. There was only one picture, a rough pencil sketch of a woman. I realized with a start that it was me.

He was very embarrassed now. "Now you know why I didn't want to show it to you."

"But why not? It's very good." I couldn't understand why he hadn't shown it to me. Clearly he had intended to keep it to himself. But why? He was here, in his own way, for the same thing I was. Why wouldn't he make use of such an effective lure?

"I sometimes sketch when I come to places like this. Gives me something to do when I'm by myself, you know?" He spoke hurriedly to cover his embarrassment. "Besides, what with all the costumes, I thought I might come across something really interesting to draw."

"I see." I examined the sketch closely. The way the woman in the drawing held her head gave her an air of intelligence. Her lips were not the sensual fantasy I expected, but rather soft and kind. Most striking were her eyes. They were dark and tired. I looked so ... human.

The music faded out then and the lights came up on the floor. Without the anonymity to keep them going, people wandered back to their table or off to get a drink.

"How are all you demons out there tonight?" the DJ asked, much too loudly and cheerfully. "You all look like hell!"

There were a few answering howls and shrieks from some of the more inebriated patrons, and quite a few obscenities as well.

"We'll get back to the dancing for all you boys and ghouls out there in just a couple minutes."

"Jesus," Jerry said, shaking his head. "Boys and ghouls."

"First off, I want to remind you that Rock 109 will be sponsoring a sneak preview of the new movie *Hellbeast* this Thursday at eight o'clock at the Cinema Seven. I've seen some reviews, gang, and this one's supposed to be scarrrry! Also, don't forget to vote for your favorite demon tonight. I've got the ballots, so just come on over to the booth and get them. You've still got half an hour to get your votes in. Remember, the winner of tonight's contest will take home one hundred dollars and will be automatically registered for Rock 109's trip to Hawaii. All right, enough talk. Let's get back to raising hell!" Thankfully, the music started. It wasn't long until the dance floor was filled again.

"So why didn't you come in costume?" Jerry asked. "Not in the mood?"

I shrugged. "I couldn't think of anything."

I hadn't known about the contest beforehand. I wander at random, following my instincts. Just before the club opened, I chose my form and changed from shadow and mist into the woman Jerry saw before him. If I had known about the contest, I could have created a costume from my substance, as I did the blouse and jeans. Perhaps in my younger days, such a joke would have appealed to me. Now it seemed like more effort than it was worth.

"I really like your outfit," I said. "It's very clever."

"Thanks."

"Where'd you get the idea from?"

"I work at a video store, so I see a lot of movies. I love those old deal-with-the-devil flicks. You know, the ones where Satan's always very urbane and dapper? I get a kick out of seeing the Prince of Darkness portrayed as a kind of insurance salesman."

I giggled, but this time it was only half-affected. There was no devil, not in the form Jerry mimicked. But there were myself and others of my kin. And urbane and dapper we are not.

The conversation lagged for a moment, and we took the opportunity to finish off a little more of our drinks. "Do you really want to hang around for the rest of this contest?" I asked.

He smiled. "Well, I did go to a lot of trouble to get all decked out. Took me almost ten minutes."

"I was thinking maybe we could go someplace and talk."

"What's wrong with talking right here?" His smile faded just a bit. "Look, I like you Lana, but ... not so fast, okay?"

"Sure." I forced myself to relax and give him a smile, but inside I was furious. He wasn't ready yet, and I hadn't realized it! This had never happened before. I was so upset I nearly got up and walked away. But then I realized something. This really hadn't happened before. Once again I was living the hunt, not merely going through the motions. For the first time in ... no, for the first time, the outcome of an evening was in doubt for me. And it was exciting.

I nodded to the dance floor. "Who do you think will win?"

"The contest?" He sat his empty bottle down and looked around the room. "I don't know. Maybe that guy over by the bar, the one in the purple robe."

The man Jerry pointed to was tall, almost seven feet. He wore a robe of deepest purple, embossed with stars and silver crescent moons. His mask was pale yellow, and a single spiral horn jutted from the middle of its prominent brow. One eye hole was cut out for him to see, but the other was a rubber sculpture, torn from its socket and hanging bloodily down to the cheek.

"Why him?" I asked.

"I don't know. He just looks like a real demon, you know? I guess I think a demon should look like something scarier than you can imagine. For me, that guy comes the closest."

I nodded, wondering if Jerry would have a chance to change his mind before the night was over. I gestured to the dance floor. "What if *they* were real? Right now."

He thought about it for a moment. "This is probably going to sound stupid, but I would draw them. See, the reason I like to draw things is because, while I do it, I feel, I don't know, like I kind of get into what it is that I draw. I understand it, on a different level than the kind of understanding you get just by thinking about something or talking to someone. As just a bunch of people in costume, they're fun to look at and sketch. But if they were really demons, I'd draw them so I could understand, really understand what it was like to be one."

"What if you didn't like what you discovered?" I glanced down at his sketch of me.

"I'm not interested in liking something when I draw it. I just want to understand it."

I smiled and fingered the edge of the paper. "And what did you learn about me from this?"

"That I wanted to come talk to you."

"Come on."

"Really. You think I came over just because you're pretty? If that was all I saw, I wouldn't have bothered."

"Beauty is unimportant to you?"

He smiled. "Not at all. It's just that there are dozens of better-looking guys than me here tonight. And they were all eyeing you before I came over. Hell, most of them still are, waiting for me to strike out so they can have their shot. A girl as pretty as you are is awfully intimidating to a guy like me. I'm not exactly Mr. Universe."

"Then why did you come over?"

He picked the sketch up and looked at it. "It's hard to explain. Usually when girls as pretty as you come to a place like this, they spend all their time looking around, checking out the guys, enjoying the music, whatever. But you, well, you weren't really paying attention to what was going on around you. You were focused on what was going on inside you. Kind of brooding, you know."

I forced a laugh. "And you find that attractive?"

He put the sketch back down with a smile. "I guess. It made you stand out in a way your beauty couldn't. What were you thinking about anyway?"

I hesitated.

"Nevermind," he said. "You were probably just thinking about work or something, and I read too much into it." He tapped his fingers on the table in time to the music.

"Would you like to dance?" he asked. The question was casual. His eyes showed that he was afraid I would say no, certain I would give some apology, I already had a boyfriend, a fiancé, maybe.

"Sure."

He grinned and I found myself grinning back. He stood, took off his jacket, and draped it over the back of his chair.

He offered me his arm in a mock-gentlemanly manner. "Madame?" There was his own anticipation, his own need, not really so different from my own, beneath the word.

"Sir." I rested my hand in the crook of his arm as he led me to the floor.

The dancers moved aside, giving us a tiny space. The walls next to the sound booth were mirrored and showed the two of us in the midst of whirling and gyrating creatures. Jerry turned out to be not a bad dancer at all. I felt free to let go just a bit more, to show off a little. It had been a while since I had a chance to really cut loose on the dance floor. By this point in the evening, my escort and I have usually moved on to bigger and better things. But I was surprised to find myself actually having fun.

I found myself succumbing to the beat, losing myself in the music. The beat was in the floor, in my feet; I breathed it, tasted it, drank it in. And before me was Jerry. I began to see him, not as bone and meat, but as shifting patterns of energy, pulsing with delicious life. I couldn't stop myself any longer. I reached out and began to take him, to drain his life into myself.

Just then I caught a glimpse of our reflections out of the corner of my eye and I stopped dancing and stared. There was Jerry, slowing down as his life energy began to trickle out of his body. Around him were other dancers, most costumed, but a few were wearing regular clothing. And there, right next to Jerry, was a white-faced woman standing deathly still. But I couldn't tell her apart from any other woman on the dance floor. She was just another person in the crowd. And for a dizzying, sick moment, I asked myself: Just what am I?

But then a man in a skintight black leotard painted to resemble a skeleton whirled away from his partner and came between me and my reflection.

Jerry lost the beat for a half-second and he swayed, light-headed. I reached out to steady him. "Beer catching up to you?"

He was uncertain, confused. "I guess so."

"It'll pass. Just take it easy."

My own confusion had broken the connection before I could take more than a little of his life force. What had I been thinking of, trying to take him in public like that? But I hadn't been thinking. And with that, I had the answer to my earlier question. I was Hunger, and that's all I was. The song ended and there was a brief moment before the next one, a moment filled with clinking glass and the soft buzz of conversation beyond the edge of the dance floor. The lights dimmed and a slow song came on. Some people left the floor, while others went into their partners' arms. Still others emerged from the shadows to embrace and sway to the music.

The momentary mingling of our life forces had made it far easier to sense his feelings, and I knew that he wanted to touch me, wanted me to touch him. I placed my hands lightly on his shoulders. His hands trembled slightly as they rose to my waist. I took a half-step closer to him, and he to me. The floor seemed to flow beneath us, like we were treading lightly on the surface of a cool, tranquil lake.

Jerry pulled me closer. I could not only sense his emotions, I could feel them as intensely as if they were my own. I didn't just know his hope and excitement; they became mine. The sudden intimacy was most ... disturbing. I put a mild psychic block between us. I am Hunger, I reminded myself. Nothing else.

He pulled back and looked at me. "Are you okay?"

"Fine." He wasn't very reassured, so I pulled him close once more and let my body reassure him for me.

We held each other through the song and two more. His hair was in my face and I breathed in the dizzying aroma of maleness, of cologne and sweat. My tongue darted out of its own volition and flicked across a strand of his wet hair. I relished the taste of him. The need was full on me now.

I whispered in his ear. "Could we go get some air? I'm starting to feel a little ill."

We left the dance floor and returned to our table. "I'll be fine once I get out of here."

He nodded as he slipped into his jacket. His goatee was coming off. He pulled it free and tossed it on the table. I reached for my purse, and paused as I saw the sketch lying there. I picked it up and put it in my purse. We weaved through the tables and smoke toward the exit.

Outside, I breathed deeply. "That's much better. Thank you."

"Are you sure you're okay?"

"I guess it was just too much wine. What time is it?"

He checked his watch. "A little after two."

I sighed. "I was hoping we could get a bite to eat, but it's a little late for me. I should go back and call a cab."

"You don't have to do that. I could give you a ride home."

I smiled. "I'd like that."

We'd been driving only a few minutes when I told Jerry I was feeling sick again.

"Do you live close by?" I asked.

"About ten, twelve miles. We could be there in a few minutes. You might feel better if you could lie down for a while."

"That might be a good idea at this point."

We pulled into the parking lot of his apartment complex. He was on the second floor. I allowed him to help me up the stairs.

He opened the door to his apartment and stood back to let me enter. It was a one-bedroom, big enough for one, perhaps two when the occasion demanded it.

He shut and locked the door. "Is there anything I can get you?"

"A glass of water would be nice."

He went into the kitchen.

I heard him open a cupboard and turn on the tap. I looked around the room and realized that what I had first taken to be framed pictures were instead Jerry's artwork. A landscape, a kitten, an old man, a skyline at night.

He came back into the room and handed me my glass of water.

"I thought you were shy about your work."

"I am. These are for me. Not many people ever get to see them."

I smiled at the implied compliment. "I'm honored, sir." I took a sip of water.

"Let's go sit down," he offered.

I nodded and he led me to the couch. I drank a little more.

"I think I'm better now, Jerry. Thank you for taking care of me. You're very sweet." I leaned over and kissed him lightly on the lips.

It took him by surprise. "You're feeling better, I take it."

"I'm starting to feel all right, but I'm not sure I'll make a full recovery. Unless ..."

"Unless what?"

"Another kiss or two wouldn't hurt?"

He grinned and pulled me to him. The kiss was intense and my hunger welled up. But I held myself back. Just a little longer and it would be so much better.

He undressed me slowly, clumsily. He hadn't done this many times and his hands were unsure. His lips moved over my skin as I unbuttoned his shirt. Then I undid his belt and helped him out of his pants. We hugged, and the hunger sang within me. I could feel his own hunger calling to me.

We got down on the floor and we joined.

He was unpracticed, but what he lacked in skill, he made up for in enthusiasm. He was a rare one—totally open and giving of himself. There would be no tearing, no rending of body and spirit that makes a soul bland and tasteless. He was opening the doors for me, one by one, until he would be mine.

Right before I feed, my perceptions shift and instead of seeing a man's face, I always see the bright flare and pulse of his life force as he builds to orgasm. But it didn't happen this time. I watched, for the first time, the face of my prey. Watched him revel in his body's sensations, saw his tender expression as he kissed my neck, my face. Saw deep into his eyes as he looked into mine.

I wondered if it had been like this before. Had all their faces shown the same emotions? Had all their feelings been ... real? All night I had been thinking of Jerry as special. But what if they all had been special?

We flowed together, pulsed one against the other with building urgency. The sensations my body gave me were nothing compared to the waves of Jerry's Self which crashed into me. As he neared orgasm I dissolved the block and easily stripped away what remained of his psychic defenses.

I watched his face as his breathing quickened. His skin was flushed and I couldn't get over how alive he was. Over his shoulder, I saw one of the drawings on his wall. The one of the kitten. And I realized something. It hadn't been my lure that had drawn him to me. He had come over to my table because he had seen beyond my disguise. He had seen what no one else ever had. Me.

He held me tight as he came. His soul shone full and bright, and I reached deep to feed.

But for the first time I understood what it was that I took from my prey. I understood Life.

And I spared him.

We rested in each other's arms for a while. After a bit he asked me not "How Was Yours?" or "Was it Good?" but "How are you?"

"I'm fine."

His brow furrowed with worry. "You're crying."

"I am?" I touched my cheek and found it wet.

"Is something wrong?"

I shook my head. "Could you just hold me some more?"

I was gone by morning. I had reverted to my true form, little more than a bit of unseen fog, and slept as I drifted through towns and cities, across country sides.

I'm sure Jerry was hurt and puzzled by my absence when he awoke, but I couldn't stay with him. No matter how much I understood, I would never be more than a mockery of what he thought I was.

But I did leave him something. His sketch of me.

The next was another town, another bar. The place was seedy, the tables scarred by ancient graffiti which held the crusted black scum of years of cigarette ash and spilled beer. The body I chose that night was young and blond. I wore a tight, thin T-shirt and shorts.

The clientele could hardly be considered sophisticated. The majority of patrons were already drunk, although it was still early, and were bellowing out the words to a song on the jukebox.

A man walked up to my table. He was thin, reedy, skin weathered by time and work. He had been handsome once, before he'd seen too much of life, but he retained enough of his former looks to approach me with confidence.

"You're new 'round here, aren't you?"

"Yes, I am. Care to show me around?"

His smile became a grin. "I'd like that."

I stood. He offered me his arm and I took it. Later I tore the soul free from his body and devoured it whole. I had to look at his face the entire time, had to see his eyes as the life left them. I see all their faces now.

It goes on like that. Every night someplace else. But not always someone else. Sometimes I can't go through with it. And I've noticed I'm getting weaker.

What happens to a shark when it can no longer make itself eat? It soon dies, sinks to the bottom and is buried in mud, forgotten.

But one thought will make that long descent easier. I will not be forgotten. Not as long as there's a small, framed sketch on a wall somewhere.

COMMENTS

I wrote this story for one of my graduate-level creative-writing classes back in 1988-89 (I can't remember which year for sure). I was 24 or 25, and recently married to my first wife. PC's were still new back then, and I wrote it on some boxy black metal computer my dad gave me, with a thick glass screen and glowing green letters. I had a daisy-wheel printer which produced copy that looked as if it had been written using a typewriter, since my professors (not to mention editors) weren't fond of trying to read dot-matrix printer text. Dad got the printer for me, too. He worked repairing ATM machines, but technology was a hobby for him—his passion, really—and he always found computers and printers cheap in those days, often repairing or even building them himself. I sometimes wonder what my dad would've done if he'd had the opportunity to go to college. Would he have become an engineer? Or a computer designer? Maybe.

My inspiration for "Huntress" was twofold. I'd read an article in *Writer's Digest* about the most common clichés in horror fiction, and one of them was called The Jaws of Sex. This is a horror story where an unsuspecting victim (usually a man) is lured by person (usually a woman) into a sexual encounter. During the encounter, the woman reveals herself to be a monster of some kind and kills the man. I decided to give the cliché a go, only I'd turn it around, make the monster the main character, and see if I could make readers feel sympathy for her. My second inspiration was Suzy McKee Charnas' novel *The Vampire Tapestry*. Skip the next paragraph—which I've enclosed in brackets—if you don't want the book's ending spoiled for you.

[At the end of the novel, the vampire character comes to view his prey as people instead of food, and he can no longer bring himself to kill them. He then goes into hibernation, and when he awakens, he'll be a pure unfeeling predator again. He goes through this cycle every century or so, with no memory of his previous lives, as this is the only way he can survive.]

I decided to make my main character a succubus so she'd be more directly connected to sex than a vampire or other monster, and I decided *she* would be an *it*, a genderless being who could be either male or female, depending on a victim's sexual preference. The character would be unimaginably old, and I decided that she (the entity presented as a woman in the story) would develop empathy for humans, which would make it more difficult for her to feed, putting her existence in jeopardy. I would focus on the climactic (no pun intended) night where she finally makes a connection to one of her victims and finds out once and for all who and what she really is.

I didn't know it at the time, but what I'd done was give my story an emotional core. It was about an important struggle for the main character, one which would determine the course of her life.

Because I wanted readers to feel the most sympathy for my main character as possible, I decided to write the story in first person. For whatever reason, I tend not to use first person a lot. Probably because a first-person narrative implies the narrator lives through the story events, decreasing suspense and tension (especially in horror), and it brings up the question of who the narrator is telling the story to and why. Plus, how much time has passed between the events the narrator is describing and who they are now? If enough time has passed, you essentially have two main characters: the narrator today and their past self. These selves may have different attitudes, speech patterns, etc. Most readers don't worry about stuff like that, so when I write a first-person story, I tend not to worry about it either. I most often write in an immersive third-person point of view, which is close like first person, but there's a bit of distance there. I can kill the character, have them change into something awful at the end of the story, or have them commit a horrible act, all without worrying about how they're managing to tell this story themselves. And in third person, there's no narrator who already knows how the events of the story turned out. Imagine a first-person narrator starting out a story thusly: *This is a story about how I was almost killed by a ravenous werewolf who turned out to be my twin sister, and how I was forced to kill her in self-defense by stabbing her in the heart with a silver dagger. Poor Cecily. Anyway, my tale begins in New Orleans in 1997 ...*

(For some reason, I find first person more comfortable when I'm writing a novel than a short story. I have no idea why.)

Exposition can be a problem in first-person stories, as the narrator can deviate from relating events moment-by-moment and go into memories or longwinded explanations about people, places, how things work, etc. In "Huntress" I tried to keep the exposition focused on what my character was experiencing at that moment and have her tell readers the bare minimum of what they needed to know when they needed to know it. One of the ways I managed this was to leave much about my character vague so I wouldn't be tempted to put too much information in the story. I know she's a succubus, she's a predator, she's very old, she can present as either gender, her true form is some kind of energy, and that's about it. I focused more on how she *feels* about these things as opposed to a lot of specific detail about them. Writing instructors often tell students they need to have everything about their characters worked out in detail, but I've found that the less I know, the better sometimes, especially when writing short fiction. Plus, it allows me to keep a sense of mystery going about the supernatural. The more specific detail people use to depict supernatural events—especially when they fully explain the reasons behind them and how they work—the less magic there is in a story.

One really good thing about using first person for "Huntress" is that it kept me focused on the moment instead of rushing through events. I started college as an acting major, and one the things our instructors taught us was the importance of playing the moment, making sure that you hit each emotional beat in a scene in real time, the same way people experience life. I see so many beginning writers—and some published ones—who hurry through important moments in their stories or skip them altogether. I think using first person in "Huntress" helped prevent me from doing that.

Although sex was an important story element, I decided not to include explicitly erotic scenes. I thought detailed depictions of sex would only distract from the character's emotional journey.

I don't remember how the writing of "Huntress" went—easy, difficult, or somewhere in between—but I finished the story by the due date, and I was pretty happy with it. Creative writing classes at the college were taught by one of two professors, and they both used the same method. Students would bring a copy of their story to class, read it aloud while everyone listened, then the professor would invite students to provide feedback. When the discussion was over, the student handed the story to the professor, who would take it home, write one or two noncommittal sentences that were virtually useless as feedback, and return the story to the writer at the next class session. Several of my fellow grad students were in the class, so I knew I had friendly listeners who would give me good feedback in as kind a way as possible. But there were several students I didn't know, and I wasn't sure how the story would be received. Most of the students wrote realistic fiction. (One great thing about my undergrad and grad school creative writing professors—while they were literary writers, they never tried to discourage me from writing genre fiction.)

An aside about reading-aloud workshops. They're a convenient way to run a creative writing class—especially if you're a professor who doesn't want to take any work home to grade, and if you're a professor who doesn't want to take the time to figure out what you'll be doing in the next class. Everyone knows you're going to hear someone else read a draft aloud! No prep time, no work to grade at home … It's a sweet deal for a teacher. But the bad thing about read-aloud workshops is that you're not writing a script. You story isn't meant to be listened to. It's meant to be read silently by someone whose eyes are moving back and forth across the text. When you read aloud, no one can see the paragraph breaks, how you position dialogue, etc. And they can't stop, think for a few moments, maybe jot down a few thoughts, and then continue reading. Everyone is forced to listen to the story at the same rate of speed. And writers—especially beginners—are usually not gifted oral presenters, so in no time at all, everyone in the class gets tired of listening to students read in a monotone and spaces out. Far better for drafts to be available for students to read before class discussion of stories.

And for the poets reading this, yes, read-aloud workshops can work for poetry, especially if everyone has copies to follow along as people read. Poetry is short compared to fiction, so it doesn't take much time to read or listen to. Plus, there's a long tradition of poetry being recited or read aloud to an audience. Reading fiction aloud can work for a literary event, but as a feedback technique, it sucks.

When rereading "Huntress" for this book, I was struck by the fact that I wasn't nervous reading a story that deals with attraction and sex in front of a classroom full of people, at least half of whom were women. And I don't remember anyone reacting negatively to those aspects of the story. If I were taking a class today, I might be reluctant to read "Huntress" aloud. I'd wonder if people might think I was a creeper—an old man creeper instead of a twenty-five-year-old creeper—who gets off on reading a sex story in front of others. Maybe I overthink things now or maybe I'm just more aware of gender and sexual dynamics in group settings.

When it was my turn to read, I did my best. I had started undergrad as an acting major, so I was a decent read-alouder (at least I hope I was). I was excited to share this story with my classmates and the professor, and I was also nervous about what kind of feedback I'd get. Would they love it? Hate it? Feel indifferent toward it? (This one's the worst of the three.) My hands shook as I read (sometimes they still do when I read my work aloud), but once I finished, I was relieved and happy. I was proud of my story and I couldn't wait to hear what the others thought of it.

My friend Brad Marcum started his feedback off with a joke. "Ah yes, the old succubus-with-a-heart-of-gold story ..." As one student after another spoke, they identified the good aspects of my story and gave me suggestions for revision. Then it came time for Mary to talk. (I can't remember her real name, but who knows? It could've been Mary, right?)

"Men shouldn't write from the perspective of women," she said.

She went on to explain that since men and women's experiences were so vastly different, no man could ever write a woman's point of view effectively. I pointed out that my character was a supernatural being with no actual gender, but Mary said that didn't matter. Since she presented as a woman in the story, she was a woman. I was irritated by this. What writer wants to hear that there might be limits and boundaries on their imagination? But I thanked her for the feedback and decided to mull over her comments.

The next class, Mary read a story she'd written from the point of view of a young boy. I asked her why, if she thought men couldn't and shouldn't write from a woman's perspective, it was okay for her to write from a man's perspective.

"It's different," she said. "Woman are more empathic and insightful than men, and we can write from any point of view."

I didn't completely write off Mary's feedback on my story after that, but I had a better sense of where her comments were coming from. As another friend once put it, "There's no standard like a double standard."

As the years have passed, I've come to consider Mary's feedback on "Huntress" one of the greatest writing lessons I ever had. She got me thinking about the difference between writing straight autobiography disguised as fiction (the old "write what you know" advice) and writing outside your lived experience, sometimes extremely outside in the case of speculative fiction writers. So decades before people began discussing these issues on social media, I was already contemplating them and trying to decide how to deal with them in my own work. I decided that in the end, writers should be able to write whatever they want, but they should also be prepared for the world to react to their writing however it will. If you're a cishet middle-aged white man like me, and you do a terrible job writing from the point of view of a young black woman first realizing she's nonbinary, you'll be criticized for it, and rightly so.

I decided that since women made up over 50 percent of the human race I would alternate between male and female main characters in my fiction. It felt wrong of me not to reflect this reality in my work, and I'd lived around women my whole life. I was raised by them, grew up with them, was friends with them, and felt more comfortable in their presence than I did with men. Inwardly, I often felt more like a woman than I did a man. I've continued alternating between male and female viewpoints in my fiction throughout my career, always paying attention to reader and reviewer feedback to gauge how successful (or not) I am. Based on this metric, it seems I've done okay overall in portraying both genders.

I draw on aspects of women I know for my female characters, but I long ago realized that if I write them as people first as opposed to writing them as just a gender, their depiction works fine. Plus, I don't attempt to write stories that deal deeply with what it's like to be a woman in 21st-century America. I write horror and dark fantasy, and a woman's reaction to being stalked by a werewolf probably won't be all that different than a man's. What *is* different, however, is a particular character's reaction. How would *one* specific woman react? How about *one* specific man?

I've struggled more with whether I should write from the point of view of someone from another race, culture, or sexual identity. As the online discourse about this issue has changed over the years, so has my approach. At one point, women, BIPOC, and LGTBQ+ writers were encouraging cishet white male writers to use our platforms—fiction as well as social media—to promote diversity. I've lived most of my life in southwestern Ohio, and over the decades it's become more diverse, so by diversifying the characters in my fiction, I'd be reflecting the reality I lived in. So I did this.

I set some boundaries for myself. I wouldn't write stories that attempt to delve into the racial/cultural/gender/sexual identities of my characters. I wouldn't write about people who recently immigrated to America. I made sure my characters were at least first-generation Americans so they would've been raised in the same overall culture as I had been. And sometimes simply giving a character a name that indicated a particular background—such as Mendez—could indicate ethnicity without needing to go into detail about it.

I also decided to treat my characters as if I was the casting director for a film. If there was no specific reason why a character had to be a cishet white male, then they could be anything. If a character in a movie is a vampire slayer, and the story is more about what they do and how it affects them as a human, then any actor of any race, gender, or sexual identity could play that character. I took the same approach in my stories.

Then a few years later, the online discourse changed. People began saying that writers shouldn't write outside their own experience. If straight white male writers wrote from the point of view of a Hispanic gay woman, not only would they do a poor job and likely perpetuate harmful stereotypes, they'd take up space that an actual writer of that background could've filled. Editors could say, "We already bought a story featuring a Hispanic gay woman, so we've checked off our diversity box for this month." So the straight white male writer gets published, and a Hispanic gay woman writer doesn't.

People also said that the moment you describe someone as black or Hispanic or trans, you immediately other them in a culture that's still predominantly geared toward white straight people. Therefore writers shouldn't indicate race. Others said that if you don't indicate racial/cultural/sexual identity in your fiction, it allows readers to imagine characters however they wish. Others countered that if you do this, readers of any background will still tend to imagine characters as straight white people because that's the cultural default in our entertainment in America. And still others said that if cishet white male writers don't include diverse characters in their fiction, we erase everyone of any identity other than our own, and we end up presenting an all-white, all-straight world in our stories.

So what's the best approach? Damned if I know, and no one else does either. There isn't one ultimate correct way to depict diversity in our fiction because this issue is in flux in our world as it becomes more diverse. I try to go by the "first, do no harm" mantra. If I write outside my own perspective, I do so carefully and thoughtfully. I've also been experimenting over the last few years, writing some stories that have a more diverse cast, some that have a less diverse cast, and some where I make no mention of diversity beyond male and female designations. I'm trying to discover what approach feels best to me and works best for readers, but I doubt I'll ever settle on one specific answer. I'll likely continue to experiment with diversity in my writing until I die. I know I'll make mistakes and that readers and reviewers will let me know when I do, and I'll try to grow and improve as I continue.

Something else I learned from "Huntress" is that each editor has specific tastes and that none of them are "right," that the concept of "right" when it comes to art is a meaningless one. "Huntress" first appeared in the journal *Tamaqua* in 1990. I was teaching at Parkland College in Illinois at the time, and *Tamaqua* was the journal the English department produced. James McGowan was the editor, and he liked "Huntress," but he wanted me to add more detail and more internalizing on the character's part. I did and the story was published. A couple years later I submitted "Huntress" as a reprint to the small-press magazine *The Mythic Circle*. That editor asked me to take out everything that Jim had me put in, so the story returned to its original form, and *The Mythic Circle* published it. Which version of the story did I like better? The original was leaner and meaner, but some of the additions Jim asked me to make were good too. It wasn't a matter of *better* so much as *different*. If I strongly objected to making changes, I could've told Jim thanks but no thanks, but I'm always willing to consider editor's suggestions. Traditional publishing is a collaborative process. If I wasn't open to making changes, I'd self-publish.

In terms of inspiration for this story, I didn't draw much on my personal life. Back then, I frequented a bar called Bourbon Street, which had a large dance floor. Why I chose *Basin* to replace *Bourbon* beyond both words starting with B and having two syllables, I have no idea. Who would want to go to a place named after a bowl? I did go to a Halloween night at Bourbon Street once, and I knew I'd use that experience in a story one day. I thought I'd write about a bar frequented by real monsters and demons, but the experience was a perfect fit for "Huntress."

Writers are often tempted to make writers main characters in stories. Back in college, one of my friends sent such a story to *Asimov's Science Fiction Magazine,* and the editor George Scithers wrote back that now he had gotten "the drearily inevitable story about a writer" out of his system, he could go on to write something better. Whenever I want to write about being a creative person, I usually do what I did in "Huntress"—make the character a different kind of artist. So Jerry draws. In a story I wrote called "Preserver," the character is a collage artist. In my novel *Like Death,* the main character is a true-crime writer instead of a fiction writer. I find this a great way to draw on my experience as a creative person without resorting to the cliché of a writer writing about being a writer.

Another reason "Huntress" was so important to me was that I included it in the collection of stories that formed my graduate thesis. I had to present my thesis to my advisors and a group of friends and fellow students, and "Huntress" was one of the stories I chose to read. After the event was over, a woman I worked with at the university's Writing Center came up to me, looked at me for a moment, and then said, "You really can do this, can't you?" Normally, I might've demurred, having been raised with the midwestern belief that acknowledging anything positive about yourself was unseemly bragging, but instead I smiled and said "Yes, I can." It was my first public acknowledgement that I believed in myself as a writer, and it felt pretty damn good.

The version of "Huntress" that appears in this book is the one that appeared in *The Mythic Circle*. This is the story's first appearance since that publication.

WHAT MIGHT I DO DIFFERENTLY TODAY?

Honestly, I'm not sure. Oh, there are a lot of sentences I'd rework, and I might give Lana a previous experience where she'd almost failed to feed, so that she was determined not to see Jerry as special and had to fight to see him as merely food. That would up the tension and conflict for her, but it would also take away the newness of her experiencing empathy for the first time and make her a harsher character, one who ultimately was less sympathetic to readers. I think "Huntress" is, for the most part, fine the way it is. It does exactly what I set out to do, and while it's far from being the best story I've ever written, it's perfect for its time and place in my life.

EXERCISES

1. Take a third-person story you've written and rewrite it in first person. Which version do you find more effective? Are there things that first-person allowed you to achieve in the story that third person didn't?

2. Take a story you've written and rewrite it from the point of view of the monster (whether it's a literal monster or a human that performs the function of a monster in the story). Try to make the monster sympathetic to readers while still keeping it a monster. What had to change about the monster and story events for you do this? What were you able to keep the same? Do you think this new story works? Why or why not?

ALACRITY'S SPECTORIUM

Originally published in *Figment* (Spring 1992)

Alacrity knew what he looked like to the people strolling the fairgrounds. A middle-aged, corpulent man, whose fat was slowly being eaten away by the years and would someday be nothing but folds upon folds of loose flesh. An obese clown in a threadbare black suit and dayglow paisley tie, piggy eyes blinking behind Coke bottle bottom glasses. He stood before his small, black tent, waving his hands, shouting, sputtering cajolery in a rolling, gravely lilt.

"Ladies and gentlemen, you won't believe your eyes! Only five dollars to peer into the secrets of Dr. Alacrity's Spectatorium!"

His voice was carefully pitched to add to the tumult of the fair, to be part of the background, unobtrusive. He wasn't looking for customers, not these. He wanted to keep the crowd away. To this end, he dressed poorly, bathed infrequently, and refused to announce himself or his Spectatorium with sign or banner outside his calculatedly humble, unappealing tent. Those rare few who came in spite of his precautions inevitably demanded their money back. After all, who would pay just to look at one mirror? And a mirror perpetually in the dark, at that?

Dr. Alacrity smiled to himself. He only needed the one to draw his true customers.

A fair knows no night. Jangling rides, tents, booths, games—all festooned with harsh, fake-festive light. Dr. Alacrity always pitched his tent at the edge of the confused swirl of radiance, as further concealment and as a courtesy to his customers.

"You'll see things you've never seen before, things you thought you'd never see again!"

He was always surprised when it happened. There were no ominous hints, no cold chills, no mists, no tingling at the base of his skull. Just a quiet inquiry.

"What sort of things?"

Dr. Alacrity started, feeling breath in his ear, knowing it was impossible, for the soft, still voice came from far to his left. Out beyond where the fair lights could ever hope to reach. He shook his head and smiled. All these years catering to a select clientele and he still acted like a mark sometimes.

"All manner of sights, designed to dazzle and astound." He spoke in his real voice, low and gentle. No need to bark now. His potential customer could hear him quite easily. And persuasion wasn't necessary, either. The Spectatorium sold itself. To the right people.

The night parted and a woman stepped forth. There was nothing remarkable about her. There never was. She was small and frail. Young, barely more than a girl. Mousey brown hair. Drawn face. Blank expression. But alive, cutting eyes. She wore a tattered gray sweater and old, faded jeans. She looked like a runaway, a homeless child.

But Dr. Alacrity was a master of mirrors. He knew images for what they were. Illusions, all.

He made a slight bow, all he could manage with his bulk.

"Welcome." He smiled, maintaining professional composure although his pulse raced. No matter her form, he told himself to remember what she was. Years ago, while working with a rag-tag circus, he had known a one-armed lion tamer. Over a beer one night he had told Dr. Alacrity the secret to working with dangerous animals is not to forget. "Forget what?" Dr. Alacrity asked. "Anything," the lion tamer answered bitterly.

She came closer, her malnourished, sad eyes doubtful. "The stories I've heard. Are they true?" Her words were like distant wind, gentle, but with the potential for wildness and sudden violence. Or was it only his imagination? That was the trouble with illusions. You could never quite tell which were yours and which were theirs.

"Word of mouth—the best advertising money can't buy." When he saw she wasn't amused, he dropped his smile. "Yes, they are."

He felt a hint of tension in the air, the sign of a struggle that would be imperceptible to anyone who didn't know her kind. The struggle to keep from hoping too much.

"Yes, indeed. It's all here. Everything you've heard about."

Her eyes narrowed. "Everything? Forgive me if I tell you I find that hard to believe."

Dr. Alacrity's smile didn't falter. He'd heard it all before. "Why not go in and see for yourself?"

She swiveled her head toward the fair, ostensibly taking in the people laughing and talking as they walked lazily from booth to ride, kids chasing each other, begging their parents for money. But he knew she was really sneaking a quick peek at the tent flap as her eyes moved past it, trying to determine something from the thin crack of darkness, not wishing to display too much interest.

Her gaze returned to him. "And the price?"

"Also as advertised." He drew the tent flap aside to reveal a solid wall of unbroken blackness.

She didn't move. Her eyes grew wide, pupils large, drinking in the darkness, trying to see.

"There's nothing to be afraid of." He smiled. "Satisfaction guaranteed."

Her expression didn't change in the slightest but her eyes grabbed his and held them. "What makes you think I fear you?"

Dr. Alacrity forced himself not to recoil from the anger in her eyes. "You have no reason at all to fear me. Your people come from all over the world, often traveling great distances, enduring great hardships. And when they get here, they hesitate. For all sorts of reasons I probably can't imagine. But if I were to hazard a guess, I'd say they were afraid of the past."

"What's to fear? The past is dead."

"Not in my Spectatorium it isn't."

She hesitated for a long moment before speaking again. "And if this turns out to be a fraud?"

Dr. Alacrity's smile contained no humor. "You could always request your money back."

She laughed, pointed teeth flashing briefly in the shadow of her mouth. "All right, then. After you, my dear Doctor."

"How kind." He forced a chuckle and was swallowed by the darkness of the tent.

The tent was completely absent of light as the inner recesses of the Earth itself. Even when the flap was wide open on noon of a July day, no light could enter the tent. The mirror would not permit it.

He couldn't see her, but he heard the tent flap rustle closed as she entered.

"Is this it?" From outside they could never see into the tent, but once inside, they had no trouble. The mirror, again. "It's nothing but an old, propped up wardrobe mirror. A trick!"

Her anger was genuine, but he knew it masked disappointment. He heard nothing but suddenly her small hands bit into the flesh of his arms.

"Liar." She said it softly, and that made it worse. He could hear the wet sounds of her tongue and lips working, imagined her teeth bared in the darkness. Her breath was the muted scent of ancient spices.

"If I were a liar, I assure you, I would have been fertilizer long before this. Extremely dry fertilizer."

He heard the smooth, moist pull of skin as she smiled, the gentle creak of vertebrae as she nodded. "True." She took a deep breath and let it out slowly, releasing her anger, and his arm as well.

"What should I do?"

Dr. Alacrity ignored the pain of bruised and broken flesh. He'd suffered much worse. "Treat it as you would any mirror. Stand before it and look deep."

She didn't move. "But it isn't just any mirror."

"No. For my kind this mirror is dead. But for yours it is gloriously alive."

How, how, always how. They found it so hard to believe in wonders other than themselves. "This mirror is unique in all the world. Normal mirrors reflect light. But this, my masterpiece, reflects only darkness. It can show me nothing. But it will show you ... you. Isn't that enough?"

She didn't say anything for quite a while. He was beginning to think she had silently slipped out of the tent when she said, "Yes. Enough." There was a sharp intake of air and he knew she had stepped in front of the mirror.

There was silence for a time. He imagined her, not six feet away, standing before the glossy surface, scrutinizing every feature, examining every pore. Remembering, and memorizing for the future.

Dr. Alacrity didn't know how long they stood there. Some looked only moments before leaving, most stayed an hour, two. Finally, after a very long time, he asked softly, "Is it as you recall?"

Her reply was long in coming. "I ... believe so."

Poor child. It had been too long for her. "You can compare if you like."

"What do you mean?"

"Darkness can sometimes reflect more than light. Look again."

She gasped. "It's ... me."

Dr. Alacrity grinned at the almost girlish surprise in her voice. He knew she now gaped at a young girl in a hoopskirt or dingy serving girl's dress. Perhaps Egyptian finery or even animal skins. It didn't matter. It was her. Before.

The quiet lasted a very long time and was finally broken by a series of soft, breathy sobs. Her folk could produce no tears, but it didn't matter. The girl in the mirror had plenty for both of them.

After a time the sobs ended. "I believe I'm finished. Thank you."

Dr. Alacrity hesitated. "There's one more image. But not everyone chooses to view it."

"What is it?" Her voice was young, eager, an echo of the girl in the mirror. "I want to see everything!"

"My mirror displays three images. That which is, that which was, and that which is secretly longed for."

"But there's nothing else that I ..."

He knew then she realized what the last image was. They all longed for the same thing, deep down.

"The mirror can show me what it's like ... to rest?" She was no longer eager.

"More than just show. My mirror can make it a reality. If you so choose."

She was quiet for a moment and he knew she was staring at the mirror, trying—like she did outside—to see. "What's it like?"

"Gentle. Quiet. No burning sun, no sharp wood. They just slip away. Some say nothing. Many thank me."

She sighed and at that moment he wouldn't have believed she was one of them. It was a long, tired sigh. A human sigh. "If only it could make the second image real."

Dr. Alacrity said nothing. They all wished it could be so. He did too, but the mirror ... was the mirror. There was nothing he could do. He gave her some time to think out of respect, then cleared his throat. "I hate to bring this up just now, but if you do choose to see the last image, there's the matter of, ah ..."

"Your payment." Her voice was old and knowing now. It made him feel like a child. "Yes, I suppose you could hardly get it after, could you?"

"I'm sorry to mention it, but ..."

"Not at all. I understand."

He knew she did and felt cold inside. He heard the whisper of nail against flesh, and she offered him her warm, sweet, wet wrist.

When he was finished, he dabbed his mouth with a handkerchief. "Have you decided?"

He could almost see her in the darkness, standing before the mirror, leaning close, reaching out her hand and almost touching the surface, fingertips a hair's breadth away from the smooth ebony glass. Hesitating, hand trembling, for an instant that would live in her memory, like her, forever.

"Not tonight. Let the darkness hold onto some secrets for now." The flap opened and closed as she departed. He followed, stepped out, eyes dazzled by the fair lights. He shielded them with his hands, blinked, trying to catch a last glimpse of her, but she was gone.

He called out into the night. "You're welcome to come back anytime you long for a taste of what was! You can always find me! Just follow the smell of corn dogs, cotton candy, and money!"

A distant laugh floated back on the breeze. But it was strained by the knowledge that the last image would always be waiting for her inside the Spectatorium, inside the mirror.

"Boys and girls, ladies and gentlemen! Sights to thrill your eyes and chill your souls! Only five dollars! That's a mere twenty quarters! Fifty dimes! One hundred nickels! Five hundred pennies!"

The endless parade of people passed by, not the least bit interested in Dr. Alacrity's Fabulous Spectatorium, which suited him just fine. Oh, they looked sideways at him sometimes, then walked off, laughing. He knew how they saw him, an aging fat man, mounds of flesh now, but someday nothing more than a ton of baggy wrinkles draped loosely around an old, tired skeleton.

Dr. Alacrity smiled. Not him. Never.

COMMENTS

I don't remember where I got the idea for this story. I think I came up with the concept of a mirror that reflects only darkness first, and then developed characters and a plot that went along with it. There's definitely some Ray Bradbury influence here in the title and the carnival setting, and a bit of Mr. Dark in Dr. Alacrity. I chose the name *Alacrity* because I liked the sound of it, but I invented the word *Spectatorium*. I wanted something that sounded like it belonged to the late 19th century, and I think it fits. I remember going through a print thesaurus (no Internet yet) looking up various words associated with *mirror, reflection, sight, exhibit,* etc. and eventually cobbling together *Spectatorium*. I imagined the dark mirror standing by itself in a tent filled with darkness, and I was quite taken with the image. A poet friend of mine once told me that I wrote using "the logic of the image," and that's been true throughout my career. Maybe it's because I drew a lot as a kid and contemplated a career as a visual artist for a time. Or maybe it's merely a result of growing up in such a visual-oriented culture. Whatever the reason, I often begin short stories with some kind of image, whether it's based on something I've witnessed in the real world or something that pops into my head seemingly from nowhere. I write these things down, these days using the notepad app on my phone, and when it comes time for me to work on a story, I go through the list and see if anything on it resonates with me. I'll often use three elements to create a story: a strange/interesting image, an unrelated event from my own life, and an unrelated emotional core drawn from my experience, but often disguised in the story. This technique has served me well over the years, but in "Alacrity's Spectatorium" I only used an image. I hadn't learned yet how to tap into my own life, my own *self* for story material.

About a year after writing "Alacrity's Spectatorium," I realized that I needed to learn how to write *my* stories, *Tim Waggoner* stories, but I had no idea what that might mean. So I bought a handheld tape recorder and a bunch of cassettes, and began a long project of introspection. My then-wife and I lived in Vincennes, Indiana. She was working at her first full-time job as a psychologist, and I was teaching only one night class at the local community college. I had a lot of time on my hands during the day, so I would walk around our apartment and talk into the recorder about my life past and present, trying to drill down into the bedrock of who I was and what my unique perspective on life might be. I talked about everything and anything, allowing myself to express any thought or feeling, even my darkest and most shameful ones, things I'd never want anyone to know. I filled up a dozen tapes front and back, and I still have them today. I've never listened to a single one of them. The process of recording them was the most important thing. It was like self-therapy, and I found it extremely useful. I don't know if I'll ever listen to those tapes. I'm currently in the process of preparing my writing materials for donation to a university archive, and I'm contemplating sending the cassettes. I doubt any future scholars will ever use the material I donate, but when I imagine someone finding and listening to those tapes someday, I wonder what they'd make of twenty-seven-year-old Tim's ramblings. This process resulted in a huge leap forward for me, and I urge any writer reading this to give it a try—whether you audio record or write your thoughts down—and see what it does for you.

"Alacrity's Spectatorium" eventually appeared in a small-press magazine called *Figment*, edited and published by Barb and J.C. Hendee, who would go on to write many well-regarded fantasy novels. I've connected with them on social media but never met them in person in the thirty-one years since this story was published. Maybe we'll finally meet at some convention down the road. The small-press scene in horror wasn't as big then as it is now. There was no print-on-demand technology, no ebooks, no Amazon, but there were still a decent number of SF/F/H small-press magazines to submit to. There are two basic submission strategies when it comes to traditional publishing: start at the top or start at the bottom. You rank your preferred markets from your absolute dream markets down to ones that you'd be happy—or at least not unhappy—to see your work in. How you rank them is up to you. The highest markets could be the ones you like the best, the ones that pay the most, the ones that have a reputation for literary quality, or ones with the highest circulation. If you start submitting to your very best markets first, you're also guaranteed to get rejected, but when your story is finally accepted, you know it's the highest market you could hit. If you start at the bottom, your work is more likely to be accepted sooner, but you'll have no idea how high a market you could've reached since you stopped before you got there. Sending to lower markets can work well to boost a writer's confidence and help them build a list of credits. If you're lucky enough—or talented enough—selling your work to higher markets can get you noticed by readers and critics and build your career faster. Neither way is necessarily better. It depends where you are at any given point in your career and what you think works best for you.

During the early 90's, there weren't any higher-level magazines regularly publishing horror. They died when the horror boom of the 80's went bust. So small-press markets were the only choice. I liked submitting to them because they were more open to working with newer writers, and I was more likely to get a personalized rejection that provided editorial feedback on why my story wasn't chosen and how I could improve it. I also figured that I'd get experience with publishing and working with editors, and all of that was more important to me than how much money (if any) I made or how many copies of the magazine were printed. I don't think this basic attitude has ever changed for me. I'm always more interested in what I can learn from a writing and publishing experience than I am anything else (although I'm still happy to cash the largest checks I can get!).

When I received my contributor's copy, I saw that the editors had written in their intro to the story that I'd "snuck up on us with this one through the door labeled 'something new on a well-known theme.' And of course we couldn't resist it." This floored me. I hadn't considered that I had taken an old trope and turned it around to create a different take on it *and* that this approach was something editors were looking for. I just had an idea for a story, and I wrote it. This taught me a hugely important lesson about writing stories for both readers and editors. If you can find a way to take a well-known trope in your genre, such as vampires casting no reflections, and reverse it—what if there was one mirror in the world that could show a vampire's reflection?—you can create a story that's both familiar and original, and it'll be more likely to sell. It's a technique I've used ever since I wrote "Alacrity's Spectatorium," and I'd wager that most of my nearly 200 story publications, as well as a good number of my novels, owe their existence to this technique. When I give writing workshops or write how-to articles or books, I regularly advise people to rework well-known, overused, and tired tropes to give them new life.

Unlike "Huntress," "Alacrity's Spectatorium" isn't written with a close point of view. I stay in the moment, and there's an emotional core to the story, but this is primarily an idea story. The most important element is the dark mirror that can show a vampire's reflection. I could change the specific characters and change the setting and the basic idea would remain. Often idea stories are shorter (it doesn't take long to demonstrate an idea) and they don't go into the same kind of immersive, emotional detail as other stories (because then the detailed characterization would loom larger than the idea, and it would end up making the story longer). Plus, since I didn't want to forecast the ending, it was necessary not to go too far into Alacrity's point of view, or so I thought at the time.

While rereading the story in preparation for this book, I found that I still like it, although I have some issues, which I'll address below. I was surprised how much of it I remembered, but then, there's really not much to it, is there? It is a simple idea story after all.

This is the first appearance of "Alacrity's Spectatorium" since its original publication in 1992.

WHAT MIGHT I DO DIFFERENTLY TODAY?

Aside from reworking some of the prose, I'd reexamine the idea. A lot of it doesn't make sense to me now. If someone had created a mirror like this, why travel with a carnival? If word has gotten around the vampire community that such a miracle existed, wouldn't they travel to you? You could buy a house and live there while vampires came knocking at your door. And if for whatever reason you do decide to travel with a carnival—maybe vampires are more comfortable approaching you outside of a town—why would you only have one tent with one attraction in it that only works for vampires? I originally liked the image of one mirror standing in a tent, and I still do, but wouldn't Alacrity have another tent with attractions to make money from humans too? I doubt vampires visit him regularly, so even if he didn't care about making money, he'd still need to justify his attraction's existence to the rest of the carnival folk, especially if he didn't want to rouse any suspicion about what his true motives were.

Both Alacrity and the unnamed vampire aren't well-developed as characters. As I said earlier, too much characterization and character background can work against idea stories, but I'd be curious to see how the story would change if both characters were more fully developed. I'd consider writing the story from the vampire's point of view too, since she's the one who goes through an emotional journey, not Alacrity. If you're ever having trouble deciding who the main character in your story should be (or who the main character should be in a particular scene in a novel), ask yourself who has the most emotional investment in the events, who has the most to gain or lose emotionally? Most likely, that person is your main character.

One thing I question now is why I decided to depict Alacrity as fat. It doesn't seem to add anything to the story, unless I meant to hint that he's well fed thanks to his vampire clients, even if the blood he drinks prolongs his life instead of adding physical mass to his body. It might have been a way to indicate another level of grotesqueness and help create an overall atmosphere that things aren't quite right in this setting. Physical differences used to be—and often still are—used in horror as main elements or just as "seasoning," and I picked up on this and incorporated it into my work without much thought. Now, of course, people are much more aware of society's prejudices toward physical differences and differences in physical and mental abilities. We know better, or at least we should, than to use such differences as a way to depict some sinister Other that our heroes need to defend themselves against. Physical distortion has been a way to symbolically differentiate between Good/Evil and Normal/Abnormal in myth and folklore for thousands of years, and only within the last few decades have we recognized the harm this can do to real human beings in the real world. Was I fatphobic back then? My mother was fat, and our father forbid any kind of mention—even a hint—about her weight or anyone's weight. If someone made a fat joke on TV we'd all freeze, fearing that it made our mother feel bad and not knowing what we should do. I was never ashamed of her weight. She was just Mom to me. But she was a depressive agoraphobic who experienced regular fainting spells that were never adequately diagnosed by doctors. I'm sure her weight was a major reason she didn't want to leave the house, especially since she'd been a young woman in the 1950's, when there was such a strong emphasis on women being thin. (That emphasis is still with us today, but people are working to counter it now in ways they didn't back then.)

When I was young, I was super-thin, to the point where people thought I looked strange. (That was many, many years ago. I'm not thin now!) I know what it's like to have people judge me by my appearance, even if only in a small way, and I try to remember that feeling when I interrogate whether there are ableist elements in my fiction. While I try to avoid ableism in my horror fiction, that doesn't mean all my characters are beautiful and in peak physical health. And if someone gets turned into a monster, they'll look like a monster. But I try my best not to use physical appearance or ability as an indicator of evil/weirdness in my stories. Today if I wrote "Alacrity's Spectatorium," I wouldn't use weight in my depiction of Dr. Alacrity. And if you don't already, I urge you to consider how you use physical appearance/ability in your own work.

EXERCISES

1. Make a list of common horror tropes, especially ones you're sick of. Now make another list using the same tropes, only this time find a way to reverse them or put a new spin in them. Select an idea from the second list and write a story based on it. How did it turn out? How is it different (if at all) from what you usually write?

2. Go back through some of your old stories (whether published or not) and see how you used descriptions of physical appearance/ability/mental and emotional capabilities and health, etc. Did you use any like I used weight in "Alacrity's Spectatorium?" If so, can you think of ways to revise the story to avoid ableism? (And don't beat yourself up if you did. Just try to do better.)

MR. PUNCH

Originally published in *Young Blood* (Zebra Books 1994)

Mr. Punch swung the bat one more time, just to be sure the Judy was dead, then stepped back to admire his handiwork.

"Well, I declare now, that very pretty!" he said in a jolly voice. The Judy's head was nothing more than red and gray jelly and matted blonde hair now, her once beautiful face a memory. But Mr. Punch hadn't been fooled by her exterior. She was a Judy, all right. Inside, they all were.

Applause rang through his mind and he bowed to the right, then the left, and then to the middle, so low that the corners of his dark gray trench coat swept the floor. Tonight had been an especially wonderful performance, and it took some time for the applause to die down.

When the audience had finally finished, Mr. Punch went into the bathroom and turned on the light. He set his bat in the corner and checked himself in the mirror. Blood speckled his grotesque features. He pursed his thick, bloated lips in distaste and turned on the water. He sang as he washed.

> Mr. Punch is one jolly good fellow
> His dress is all scarlet and yellow,
> And if now and then he gets mellow,
> It's only among his good friends.

Mr. Punch washed his thick brow, hook nose, and jutting chin, then grinned at himself in the mirror.

"You one handsome fellow, Punch!"

His reflection winked in agreement.

He toweled his face dry, then wiped the gore off his bat. He didn't worry about his clothes; he always wore his trench coat and a black shirt underneath. At night, they didn't show the blood, if he was careful to keep to the shadows. And he always was.

He would've preferred the traditional scarlet and yellow, but sometimes tradition had to give way for convenience.

Mr. Punch was returning to the Judy's living room to bid her a fond farewell (and perhaps do a curtain call or two) when he heard a *scritch-scritch-scratching* at the door.

He froze, gripping his bat tight.

Scritch-scritch-scratch. Scritch-scritch-scratch.

A dark, muffled giggle drifted through the door and Punch knew who was on the other side.

It was the Devil, come for him at last.

Once, Mr. Punch had been an ugly little boy whose mother took him to a Renaissance festival at the county fairgrounds. He hadn't wanted to go, but she insisted it would be ed-u-ca-tion-al for him. She was forever searching for ed-u-ca-tion-al activities and events to take him to. He'd asked her why once, and she said because he wasn't going to get anywhere in life on his looks. He didn't like going out in public, didn't like the way people stared at him, how other kids would laugh and point, how parents would whisper things to each other like "How could such a pretty woman have such an ugly child?" and "Maybe he's adopted." He'd much rather stay home and watch cartoons, but ever since his dad left his mother was the boss and he did what she said. Or else. So he went, kept his face down as they walked, and was bored out of his mind.

That is, until his mother dragged him over to where a group of people sat before a large, brightly painted box with a big square cut out in the middle.

They settled down on the grass. "Sit up straight," his mother hissed, even though they were sitting cross-legged and everyone else was slouching. She never punished him in public. But when they got home ...

He did as she ordered.

Then the Funny Man stepped out from behind the box. He was dressed old-fashioned, like the other performers at the festival. He was all beard and bony angles, with a gap-toothed grin and wide, wild eyes that were more than a little scary.

"Good day, t'ye, little ones? Welcome to Bright's Puppet Show!"

The Funny Man swooped down to execute a deep bow and nearly fell over. The people laughed, including his mother, so he knew it was okay and joined in.

The Funny Man straightened and continued his spiel. "On this fine day, we have for ye the story that's been the favorite of folk both little and big for centuries: the saga of Mr. Punch."

He'd never heard of Mr. Punch, but from the way the people in the audience applauded and his mother smiled, he figured it was a good thing.

"Now before we begin, I want to stress something for the little ones out there," the Funny Man said. "Mr. Punch is a funny fellow, and it's right fine to laugh at him. But always remember: we laugh at Mr. Punch because he's a *bad* man who does *bad* things. We don't want to be like Mr. Punch, do we?"

A number of children shouted, "NO!" He looked at his mother, but she didn't give him an approving nod, so he kept quiet.

The Funny Man clapped his hands together and rubbed them vigorously. "All right, then? Without further delay, let the show begin!"

He ducked behind the box. Lively merry-go-round music started from somewhere back there, muffled and distorted.

And then the song began.

"Mr. Punch is one jolly good fellow ..."

As soon as the song was over, a tiny figure in scarlet and yellow appeared. Everyone cheered.

When the little boy saw what the puppet looked like, he grinned in delighted surprise.

Scritch-scritch-scratch. Scritch-scritch-scratch.

Mr. Punch felt a line of cold sweat roll along his spine. He stood gripping his bat, trying to decide what to do.

Scritch-scritch-scratch. Scritch-scritch-scratch.

He went to the window. No fire escape. And the apartment was too high up for him to jump.

He looked to the phone on a stand beside the couch. But there was no one he could call. No one who would help Mr. Punch, because Mr. Punch was a bad man.

Scritch-scritch-scratch.

Mr. Punch squeezed his bat tight and tip-toed around the Judy's body to the door. He pressed a malformed ear to the wood and listened.

No more scritch-scritch-scratchings.

He imagined the Devil crouching on the other side, giggling silently to Himself over Mr. Punch's dilemma.

"Punch not like this," he whispered. This was the moment he had dreaded for years, ever since the day he had first taken up his bat and taught his first Judy a good and proper lesson. And he had taught many more since. For was he not Mr. Punch, the Devil's master? He screwed up his courage, took a deep breath, and threw open the door.

The audience gasped in terror, then laughed in relief. The hallway was empty.

He looked both ways, just to be sure. Then he grinned, flushed with triumph.

"Devil so scared, he run away!"

And speaking of away, it was time for him to be going. He had taken a terrible chance following this Judy all the way up to her apartment, but it had been too long and he couldn't help himself. He managed to get the first blow in while they were still in the hallway, striking from behind while the Judy was fumbling with her keys. She had crumpled without a sound, and he'd dragged her into her apartment to finish the job.

So far he had been lucky, but that was only to be expected. After all, he was Mr. Punch. Still, there was no sense pushing his luck. He tucked the bat in the special long pocket he had sewn into his trench coat and closed the door behind him.

He took the stairs to avoid meeting anyone, whistling the Punch song as he took them two at a time, his shoes clanging on the metal, the sound echoing up and down the stairwell.

But then there was another sound coming from below him. A distant, high-pitched giggle.

He stopped so suddenly that he had to grab the railing to keep from falling. He listened and the giggle came again, a bit closer this time, followed by a sound that could only be a pair of hooves ringing off the stairs.

The Devil hadn't been so scared after all.

The little boy enjoyed the play very much. Punch was a very funny fellow. He chuckled when Punch threw his baby toward the audience, and laughed out loud when he beat his wife Judy with his big stick until she died.

But the best part came at the end.

Everyone but Punch was either dead, wounded or driven away by the threat of his big stick. Punch was tra-la-lahing in victory when there was a POOF! followed by a puff of foul-smelling yellow smoke.

It was the Devil.

He was quite a sinister Devil, all fiery red skin and sharp black horns. And a leering smile full of sharp teeth.

The little boy couldn't take his eyes off that smile.

"Oh, dear me!" Punch said, quivering in terror. "There he is, sure enough. Sweet, kind Devil, me never did you any wrong, but rather all the good that me could!"

The Devil advanced, pitchfork held out before Him.

The little boy bit the inside of his cheeks and silently urged Punch to run.

"Me don't want to keep you, Mr. Devil. Me know you have a great deal of business when you come to Londontown."

The Devil continued toward Punch.

"Oh, dear, what will become of me?"

"Run!" the little boy urged silently. But Punch just stood there trembling as the Devil drew near and then suddenly hit Punch on the head with his pitchfork with a solid CLACK!

The audience laughed. But not the little boy.

"Ow! Why you do that, Mr. Devil? How 'bout we be friends?"

The Devil hit Punch again. CLACK!

Punch was getting angry. "You must be one stupid devil not to recognize your best friend when you see him? Hit me, will you? Well, then, let us see who is the best man—Mr. Punch or the Devil!"

Punch attacked the Devil with his great stick, and the Devil fought back with his pitchfork. At first it looked like the Devil would win, but Punch felled the Devil with a series of mighty blows. The Devil slumped lifeless over the edge of the box.

The little boy clapped his hands and cheered, ignoring his mother's disapproving scowl.

Then Punch put his stick up inside the Devil puppet and twirled him around in the air.

"Hurrah, hurrah!" Punch shouted. "The Devil's dead! Now we can do as we please!"

The music came up as the show ended and applause filled the air. The little boy grinned, drinking in the applause as if it were for him. His mother, frowning her Things-Have-Not-Gone-As-I-Planned frown, yanked him to his feet.

"Time to go," she said coldly.

He wanted to go over to the box and see the puppets up close, maybe even ask the Funny Man if he could touch Punch. But he knew better than to argue with his mother, so he went.

Mr. Punch reached into his coat and took out his bat. The tangy smell of dried blood filled the air, mingling with the growing stench of sulfur.

The giggling rose up from beneath him, much closer now.

"Oh, dear me," Mr. Punch whispered.

The sound of hoof on metal grew louder.

He could feel the audience holding its breath in suspense.

Mr. Punch had performed his play dozens of times, and although he had waited for Him, not once had the Devil shown up. It had gotten to the point where he had begun to think that maybe there was no Devil. Oh, how foolish of him to doubt!

Mr. Punch forced himself to lean over the edge and look down the stairwell. He thought he could make out a shadowy form below. The sulfur smell was so strong now that he had to keep swallowing to avoid gagging.

Why had the Devil shown up now? And why here, in the stairwell, instead of on a proper stage?

And then the answer came to him: because the Devil knew He couldn't beat Punch fairly. The only way He could hope to win was to cheat.

"You one sneaky Devil!" Punch called out. "But Mr. Punch more sneaky yet!"

And he turned and hightailed it up the stairs. The Devil followed, hot on his heels.

The audience burst into applause.

On the way home, the little boy stared out the window at the passing scenery, replaying the final moments of the play over and over in his mind.

"That last part was a lie," his mother said after a time.

He looked at her, because if he didn't, she'd get mad.

"That part about Punch killing the Devil. It wasn't true. Nobody can kill the Devil." She paused. "Except God, I suppose."

He nodded, because he knew she expected it. In his mind, he watched Punch hit the Devil again and again.

"Do you understand?" She took her eyes off the road long enough to give him an I-Mean-Business look.

"Yes, Mother." He watched Punch twirling the dead Devil over his head, heard the audience clapping like thunder.

She must have believed him because she didn't punish him when they got home.

Eventually he did do something wrong and was punished, but he didn't mind. He took the insults and blows, all the while hearing the roar of laughter and applause instead of the sound of the hairbrush striking his flesh and the terrible awful sound of his own mother calling him names like *freak* and *wretch*.

Then one year, when he was old enough and strong enough, he worked extra hard at being a good boy all year long so he could ask for something special for Christmas. And since he had been an extra-extra good boy, he got it.

Thirty seconds after he unwrapped his new baseball bat, his mother was dead.

He looked down at her lifeless form and grinned. "What you think 'bout that, Judy?"

There was no reply, save the swelling, earth-shaking approval of the audience. Mr. Punch took his first bows.

He burst onto the roof, chest heaving, soaked in sweat. The night air, instead of being refreshing, was stale and dry. He turned and backed away from the door. He wiped his right hand on his trench coat, wiped his left, then gripped the bat with both hands.

"Come on, you old Devil!" Punch called as bravely as he could. "Now we have us a right proper stage!"

He felt strong, powerful. This was the moment he had desired and dreaded all these years. The moment when he finally killed the Devil and showed the world who was the strongest of all.

Eyes on the door, he continued backing up, step by step, expecting the Devil to come roaring toward him any second, pitchfork held high.

Then he bumped into someone. He whirled around and shrieked when he saw who it was.

"Good-bye, Punch."

Mr. Punch felt the world lurch beneath him. Then he was over the edge of the building and plummeting through space. The boos and hisses of the crowd followed him all the way to his death.

They stood arm in arm looking over the side of the building at the broken body on the street far below. The Devil licked her face, his rough, black tongue burning away the flesh-colored paint and scorching the wood beneath.

"Hurrah, hurrah! Punch is dead!" said the Judy-Who-Was-All-Judys. "Now we can do as we please!"

COMMENTS

By 1993, I'd had seven stories published in the small press. I started submitting stories for publication in the fall of 1982, so if you're a math whiz, you know that means I sold seven stories in eleven years. (I don't know how many unpublished stories and novels I'd written by then. A lot.) I was still young enough that I didn't despair about my slow progress too much. By this time, I'd heard a number of pros say that it took about ten years before you got good enough to sell consistently, and I seemed to be more or less on track. One day I saw a market listing for a new anthology called *Young Blood*, which was going to be published by Zebra Books. The premise was that the stories had to be written before the author's thirtieth birthday. Zebra wasn't a major publisher (Mike Resnick once told me it was a front for the mob), but both SFWA and HWA considered it a professional market, which meant it would be the first of three pro-level sales I'd need for active status in both organizations. Plus, I reasoned, the premise limited my competition to writers my own age or younger. No competing with established pros! When the book was published, I discovered it contained stories by Stephen King, Ramsey Campbell, Robert Bloch. Robert E. Howard, and Edgar Allan Poe—stories written before they hit thirty. I understood that's how the publisher hoped to sell the book to the reading public. Got to have at least a few big names, right? In the end, twenty-five young writers appeared in the book, including me. (And I was thrilled to have one of my stories appear next to such luminaries!) A number of the newer writers would go on to become established pros, whether in horror or another genre: Pamela Briggs, Barb Hendee, J.F. Gonzalez, Gordon Van Gelder, Brian Evenson, Sean Dolittle, Poppy Z. Brite, and Christa Faust. Not bad company for my first pro sale, eh?

I was also thrilled to be published by Zebra. They put out a shit-ton of books during the legendary 80's horror boom, and I'd read quite a few of them. Back then, I was trying to become a fantasy novelist, and I only wrote short horror fiction. Why it never occurred to me to try selling a horror novel to Zebra, I don't know. By the time I decided to give novel-length horror a try, the horror boom went bust, and publishers stopped putting out horror altogether, unless your last name was King, Rice, Straub, or Barker.

As I said, I was excited to try to get a story into *Young Blood*, and I went right to work. I don't remember how many ideas I tossed around, but eventually I wrote a story called "Yggdrasil" about a man who sacrifices people to an evil tree. (I know, I know ... *terrible* premise.) I sent it to Mike Baker, the book's editor, and he rejected it with a polite note. I knew I hadn't sent Mike my best work, and there was still a bit of time until the final deadline, so I tried again.

My first wife and I were living in Columbus, Ohio, at the time, and we'd recently gone to a small renaissance festival which I *think* was held on Ohio State University grounds. They had a Punch and Judy show, and I stopped to watch it, fascinated. It wasn't the more sanitized version I'd seen before on TV. It was the real medieval thing, far more violent and nasty, and the Devil was one of the main characters. When I was looking for a new idea for *Young Blood*, I thought of that puppet show, and I came up with the concept of a killer who thought he was Punch and all the women in the world were Judys. I imagined the killer as having a distorted face resembling Punch's, and that he'd become inspired by seeing a Punch and Judy show at a renfest, just as I had, thrilled to see someone like himself triumph, because at the end of traditional Punch and Judy shows, Punch has killed everyone, including the Devil, and is the ultimate victor. Now that I had my idea nailed down, I started writing.

This time I was determined to up my game and write the very best story of which I was capable, one that flowed out of my imagination and wasn't a mere retread of ideas I'd encountered before in books, comics, TV shows, and movies. The words poured out, but when I reached the two-thirds mark, I realized how good this story was, and I stopped writing, afraid I'd fuck it up. I don't recall how long I stayed away from my keyboard. I don't think it was very long, though, maybe just a few hours. But eventually I took a deep breath, sat back down, started writing again, and finished the story. The ending—as so many endings did and still do—came to me as I reached it, and I re-read the last few paragraphs. The ending was weird, but my instincts told me it was absolutely right for the story. I understood the story's theme then:

It was Judy's revenge on Punch for killing her so many times over the centuries, and of course, it was the revenge of all the women murdered by the killer styling himself after Punch. (This sort of dualism shows up in my work a lot. I have no idea why.)

I was feedback buddies with a college friend, Carl Grody (who was a successful freelance sports writer but wanted to break into science fiction), so I sent him a copy of the manuscript to read. By this time, I was fortunate to be in a writers' group with the fantasy novelist Dennis L. McKiernan and some other aspiring writers. I read "Mr. Punch" to the group, and when I was finished—because I had begun to lack confidence in my story—I said, "So what's wrong it?" I knew what they would say (partially because I prompted them to say it. The ending, of course. It was bizarre, surreal, and enigmatic, and while it might make symbolic and emotional sense, it didn't make literal sense. Everyone gave me ideas for how to change the story, especially the ending, and I went home determined to improve the manuscript.

I tried.

And I tried.

But every change I made only resulted in the story becoming worse. I knew the original version was the best, that it was *true*, so I told myself to forget what everyone said and send Mike the first version of "Mr. Punch," enigmatic ending and all. Carl hadn't gotten back to me with feedback on the story, but the deadline was swiftly approaching, and I'd already decided which version to send, so I didn't worry about what Carl might think. I printed out a copy and a cover letter, stuck it in a manila envelope with a self-addressed, stamped, letter-sized envelope inside for Mike's response, and popped the whole thing in the mail. (This was before editors began accepting electronic manuscripts. That transition occurred after 9/11, when editors and agents were afraid of receiving physical packages because who knew which one might be filled with anthrax or something?)

Mike loved the story and accepted it for *Young Blood*. I'd made my first professional-level sale!

Not long afterward, Carl's feedback on "Mr. Punch" arrived. My printout was dripping with red ink on every page, but it didn't matter. I'd stayed true to my artistic vision, and my story had sold. I didn't tell Carl that his feedback came too late to make a difference, though. I didn't want him to feel that he'd wasted his time reading and commenting on my story.

Several years later, I was running a writers' workshop at a Columbus con called Context (now sadly defunct). I was doing a Q&A for the participants, and my friends Gary A. Braunbeck and Charles Coleman Finley were helping me. One of the participants asked us when we knew that we had finally done it, had finally written something truly good. To my surprise, all three of us told the same story. We were writing a story, realized how good it was, stopped out of fear of ruining it, and then finally finished it. I have no idea how common this experience is, but I wouldn't be surprised to learn it happens to artists a lot.

What did I learn from writing "Mr. Punch"?

I learned to trust my instincts as a writer. I learned that my best work comes from my own weird imagination, from within me, not from outside. I'd already known how useful peer feedback could be—hell, I used it in the writing classes I taught—but I learned it can be useful for reasons other than you might think. My group's feedback ultimately helped me realize I needed to leave the story as it was. I learned not to treat feedback, even from a pro writer like Dennis, as ultimate wisdom that I must heed. Our writing group broke up when Dennis and his wife moved to Tucson, and I've never joined another. I stopped sharing work with Carl, too. I haven't gotten feedback from anyone other than agents and editors in over twenty-three years. In that time, I've traditionally published over fifty novels and close to 200 short stories, so I figure I must be doing something right on my own. (I do, however, read reviews of my work and any comments about it on social media so that I can learn how readers respond to my work, so I get feedback that way, which I can use to improve my next project.)

A word of caution about ignoring feedback, though. I don't know how many students and workshop attendees I've taught in the last thirty-five years. Maybe thousands by now. There's always someone who writes solely by natural instinct and doesn't want to compromise their artistic principles by getting feedback and revising. Maybe these writers are savants, but the odds are they're just lazy or have too large—or too small—an ego. Feedback is important when you're growing as a writer, and if later you encounter a problem with a project you can't solve, that's a good time to get feedback from a trusted peer. Whenever I get a student who doesn't want to pay attention to feedback, I urge them to do so, and if they still refuse, I tell them to start sending their work out and see what sort of editorial response they get. If they start receiving a lot of acceptances, wonderful! If they keep piling up rejections, though, they might want to rethink their stance on getting feedback. The current ease of self-publishing has circumvented this process, however. People can crap out a book in a short time and immediately upload it to Amazon. Maybe the book's good, maybe it isn't. I tell indie writers to pay attention to reader and reviewer response as well as sales, and take that feedback into account for revising your book or writing the next one.

"Mr. Punch" is one of the first stories where I used a braided narrative technique, moving between present-day scenes and past scenes. The present-day scenes often involve some of kind action (such as a character trying escape a pursuer in a nightmarish scenario), and the past scenes provide insight into the character and how they got into their current situation. This technique was so successful for me that it's one of my go-to's as a writer, and I've used it effectively in both short stories and novels. Several years back, I realized I was relying on it too much, so I made the decision to vary my story design more often. But if I need to come up with a story in a hurry, this braided-narrative technique is one of my secret weapons.

One more thing I learned from the experience of publishing "Mr. Punch." Mike Baker—who's been dead a while now—never paid any of the contributors to *Young Blood*. I didn't care about the money so much, but I was worried that HWA and SFWA would find out and decide that the sale of "Mr. Punch" didn't count toward active status. No one ever said anything, though, and I kept my mouth shut. I achieved so many goals with my story that I didn't nag Mike for the money he owed me. But I did learn to be wary of everyone in publishing after that, and that was likely the most important lesson I learned from the whole experience. There's a whole lot of disappointment in the writing life, and we need to learn to deal with it as soon as we can if we want to keep going.

One reviewer said that writers in *Young Blood* used family dysfunction and personal trauma as the real monsters in their stories, and that this was a sign of a generational shift in horror. My generation came of age in the late 70's, early 80's, and people were becoming much more aware of each other's psychological and emotional struggles, and seeking treatment for them began to be looked upon as attending to normal health needs, rather than a shameful secret to be hidden. I don't know if other authors of my generation have continued to use dysfunction and trauma as important story elements, but I certainly have throughout my career.

The word *masterpiece* originally meant a work an apprentice produced to prove to their master that they were ready to go out on their own. In that sense, "Mr. Punch" is my masterpiece.

WHAT MIGHT I DO DIFFERENTLY TODAY?

While there's some characterization to Mr. Punch, this is primarily an idea story written in a surrealistic style that I've continued to develop over the years. This was enough to get the story published, but today I would give the character of Mr. Punch more depth and try to make him sympathetic, if only to a degree. Otherwise, I don't think I'd change much.

EXERCISES

1. Think back to times you visited a carnival, fair, or circus. Pick one thing you experienced and see if you can develop a story around it. For example, once back when circuses still used elephants, I got to ride one. I've never used this experience in a story, but it's something that would work well for this

exercise. Feel free to transfer the experience to a different setting if that works better for you.

2. Plot out a short story, novella, or novel using the braided narrative technique I described above. What do you think are the strengths of this technique? Are there any drawbacks to it? If you find the outline you created was successful, begin writing the story and see how it turns out. You might end up with a new and very effective weapon in your writer's arsenal.

DADDY

Originally published in *Horrors: 365 Scary Stories*
(Barnes & Noble Books 1998)

A few days after entering the hospital, Jill and the baby, whom they'd named Seth after Jill's father, came home.

Jill looked deflated, a hollowed-out shell. The baby—Keith couldn't bring himself to think of it as Seth yet, could only think of it as *it*—looked like a tiny collection of pink-purple wrinkles.

Jill's mother had volunteered to stay over for a couple weeks to help with the baby, and Keith stayed out of their way while they talked about such arcane matters as breast-feeding versus bottle-feeding and cloth diapers versus disposable.

He tried to tell himself that it was over, that the baby was here and Jill had survived the nine months of hosting this ... thing, and that was all that mattered. But the first time he saw Jill breast-feeding it, he knew that it wasn't over, that it would never be over. The thing would feed off her—and him—its entire life. If it wasn't stopped.

That night, after both Jill and her mother were asleep, Keith stole into the nursery. He kept the light off, but he could see well enough by the Donald Duck nightlight in the wall outlet near the crib. The baby was sleeping, full of milk and contented, in its tiny blue PJ's, beneath its tiny flannel blanket. Keith looked down at the thing he had fathered. The thing that was determined to devour both him and Jill until there was nothing left.

It'll be easy, the voice said. *All you have to do is put your hand over its mouth and nose and hold it there for a few minutes. They'll put it down to sudden infant death syndrome. And you and Jill will be free again.*

Keith wondered how many of the babies who died of SIDS each year weren't really babies at all, but monsters like Seth. And how many had died at the hands of their fathers.

He reached his hand toward its face, but before he could touch it, the thing woke up and started to squall. He had to get it quieted down before Jill and her mother woke.

He picked up the baby and rested its head on his shoulder.

"Shut up," he whispered, rocking it.

The thing's mewling subsided as it snuggled against him. He felt a tingling in his chest and arm, and he knew the thing was using its powers on him, draining him, stealing his life. He was about to throw it across the room when he was suddenly filled with love for the tiny mass of flesh he held. For his son. For Seth.

He sat down in the chair in the corner and continued to rock his boy. He knew Seth had used his powers to make Keith love him, could even now feel Seth taking from him, drawing life into his tiny body. Keith would grow old and gray while Seth grew tall and strong. And one day Keith would die and Seth would live on.

As Keith felt the weariness of new fatherhood overtake him, he found that he didn't really mind so much anymore. In fact, he realized with a dull, muted horror that was already fading, it felt pretty damn good.

And in his daddy's arms, little Seth gurgled happily.

COMMENTS

In 1998, the prolific anthologist Martin H. Greenberg sold an anthology to Barnes & Noble Books. It was to be an anthology of horror flash fiction, 365 stories in all, and the idea was that busy people could read at least one story a day for an entire year. The original title was *A Horror A Day*. Marty tended to approach writers he knew for anthology submissions, but he needed a lot of stories to fill this book. So he put out a semi-public call on the HWA's private message board for members only. He needed horror stories no longer than 750 words, and he'd buy more than one story per author. What resulted was a kind of horror writer feeding frenzy, with people writing and submitting as many flash fiction pieces they could. In the end, Brian McNaughton was the champion of this unofficial contest. He sold Marty fourteen stories. I came in second place with nine stories: "Along for the Ride," "Catharsis," "Daddy," "Mirroring," "Night Eyes," "Rude Awakenings," The Secret of Bees," "Skeptic," and "A Wild Hair." "Mirroring" and "Night Eyes" appeared in my first collection, *All Too Surreal*, but the others have never been reprinted (mostly because I'm terrible about remembering to submit stories to be republished). All the stories were written specifically for *Horrors: 365 Scary Stories* (the anthology's final title)—except one.

My first daughter was born in 1995, and like every new parent, I was exhausted most of the time for the first year of her life. My wife worked during the day while I took care of our daughter, and then I taught at night, and it was my wife's turn to be with our girl. But when my daughter—who didn't sleep a lot her first year or two—would get up in the night, I had to get up with her because my wife couldn't rouse herself. I would get a few hours of sleep each night if I was lucky, then I'd be up in the morning taking care of my little one again. I was, as the Brits say, absolutely knackered all the time.

An idea came to me: What if infants were all energy vampires, feeding on their parents during pregnancy, after birth, and later as they grew? The result of this idea was a 3,000 word story called "Daddy." I submitted the story to several small press magazines without any luck, but when Marty sent out his call for horror flash fiction submissions, it occurred to me that the final scene— which ran around 750 words—could be a story in and of itself. I reread "Daddy," and sure enough, the first eleven pages weren't necessary. Everything the story needed was contained in the final scene, more so, in the final image that ended the story. I lopped off the first eleven pages, changed nothing about the final scene, sent it to Marty, and he bought it for the anthology.

I didn't feel bad about losing those eleven pages. I figured I'd had to write them to get to the last 750 publishable words. But this experience taught me an important lesson about writing short fiction. I'd learned the basic concept of starting near the end with "Huntress." But writing "Daddy" taught me to begin as close to the ending as possible, even *at* the end. And while you certainly can use multiple scenes in short fiction, a story can be more powerful if it's one self-contained scene. I also learned how little background information readers truly need to understand a story. The first eleven pages of the original version of "Daddy" contained exposition about the parents' marriage and how they were adjusting to being Mommy and Daddy. Once I jettisoned all that, I saw that it was all just needless build-up, like nervous throat-clearing before a speaker begins to talk. I also learned to focus on the primary emotional relationship in a story. The father was the one who suspected the daughter of being an energy vampire. His wife didn't. So the main emotional relationship was between Daddy and his baby girl.

That's a lot to learn from what turned out to be a 561 word story, isn't it? Truth is, while I did learn all those things from writing "Daddy," I had to keep relearning them over the years until they finally became part of my creative muscle memory. I liken the process to what a dancer or singer might go through. One day in practice they perform the right move perfectly or finally hit that note they've been straining to reach. That doesn't mean they can do so consistently yet. But at least they know it's possible, and sometimes that's all we need to keep going.

WHAT MIGHT I DO DIFFERENTLY TODAY?

If I intended to let this remain a piece of short-short fiction, I wouldn't change much. If I was reworking this exact text, I'd tinker with the beginning of it a bit. There are a couple references to material that appeared in the eleven pages that were cut which don't make any sense on their own. I might consider trying to write it from a mother's point of view and see what that does. I might expand it and follow the story from the baby's conception, through gestation and birth, through school, and on into adulthood. Then I'd have the character become a father to his own child, and the cycle continues, with his baby now draining him. I'd use a mosaic technique for this (or you could think of it as a photo album technique, whichever works for you). I'd create the story from a series of scenes that depict a different stage in the baby's development from fertilized egg to adulthood, all but the last scene written from the father's point of view. In the final scene, I'd switch to the son's point of view (the dad would probably have died by now) and show the cycle beginning anew. If I were to try making a novel from this idea, I'd develop it differently. The psychic vampire baby would be unique to the parents, and they'd seek a way to stop the energy drain on them without harming their baby, and hopefully curing the child of its parasitic condition. I might even have the appearance of vampire fetuses within women be some sort of worldwide plague or supernatural event. But since the original idea is a small, intimate one, I think it would still work best as a small, intimate story.

EXERCISES

1. Take this story's basic concept and write it from the point of view of the baby. Or you could turn the idea around and write about a situation where parents psychically feed on their own offspring.

2. Pick a room in the place where you live now (or a place where you once lived). Come up with an idea that allows you to set a story within that room. Write the story as one scene, and don't allow the characters to leave the room during the story's events. What effect did writing a story set in a confined space create? Did you find the exercise to help focus you or did you feel your imagination was too constrained?

KEEPING IT TOGETHER

Originally published in *Between the Darkness and the Fire*
(Wildside Press 1998)

Michael Dillon first noticed the crack in his wife's forehead during dinner.

Sylvia was dishing out a second helping of peas for herself, while Tammy swung more or less happily in her baby swing. The kitchen light hit Sylvia's face just right, revealing the tiny fissure that creased her otherwise smooth skin.

Tammy said ma-ma-ma, not really a word, not at five months. Just a happy baby sound.

Sylvia looked across the table at him and smiled. "More peas, hon'?"

As Michael watched, the crack widened and lengthened. He told himself that it wasn't there, told himself that real hard, and sure enough, it wasn't.

"Yeah." He held his plate out to Sylvia. It was mostly empty, save for some juice left over from the chicken and a few small clumps of mashed potato. There was a chip in the plate, but as soon as Michael registered it, it was gone.

Sylvia spooned out a healthy portion of peas for him, despite the fact that he'd already had seconds. He was about to tell her to stop when a good-sized chunk of plaster fell onto his plate, knocking it out of Sylvia's hands and sending peas flying. The plate crashed to the table and crumbled like sandstone.

Sylvia jumped back, startled, and Tammy began crying. Michael looked up at the divot in his ceiling. *Damn place is falling apart*, he thought. And then, as the realization of what that meant hit him, he thrust the thought away, buried it deep in his mind, made it never-was, or as close to never-was as made no nevermind.

Everything was fine. Everything was normal.

He smiled at his wife. "Why don't you go ahead and take the baby, while I clean up?"

"Didja get it?"

"Yeah, yeah, I got it," Michael said irritably as he lowered himself to the cool stone of the basement floor next to Barry Madden. He, like Michael, was twelve years old, and his best friend in the whole world. He dropped his dad's new *Playboy* onto the floor in front of them. "Mom nearly caught me, though." He wanted Barry to appreciate the risk he had run, but as usual Barry's mind was completely focused on the women sandwiched between the covers of the magazine.

Barry lost no time in flipping past the advertisements and articles to get to the good stuff. Michael paid no attention to the magazine, always found it and the women inside boring. Instead, he watched Barry's face, wide eyes, skin flushed with excitement, lips stretched into an eager, dirty grin. Then he looked down at Barry's crotch, and saw the bulge of his boner pushing against the fabric of his jeans. He knew it wasn't right for one guy to check out another guy's hard-on, wasn't normal. But he couldn't help himself. Michael felt his own penis begin to stiffen.

Barry looked up from the magazine and scowled at Michael. "What the hell are you lookin' at?"

Michael turned away, his cheeks burning. "Nothin'." His burgeoning erection died and fell limp.

He could feel Barry's eyes boring into him, gauging, assessing. Then Barry punched him on the arm, just a little too hard. "Fag." He said it good-naturedly, as a joke, but Michael could detect a warning in the word. Don't do that again.

And then everything returned to normal. Barry opened the centerfold of a leggy, tanned, well-endowed blonde and let out a whistle. "Man, oh, man! Look at the tits on her!"

Michael looked, trying to force himself to see whatever it was that excited Barry so, trying to make his body react like it should.

But nothing happened.

"God, I'd really love to do it to her," Barry said.

Michael tried to force enthusiasm into his voice. "Yeah, me too."

After dinner, Michael went outside to do a little yardwork. Sylvia accompanied him and stood on the porch, Tammy in her left arm, perched on her hip. The late August air was humid and clung to the skin like plastic wrap. Michael was tempted to put the work off until another, cooler day, but decided against it. He'd already let the weeds go too long as it was; if he waited any longer, they'd take over the yard completely.

As he went into the tiny two-car garage to retrieve his hoe, Michael noticed the rot eating away at the ceiling beams and concentrated, willing it to be *not*. Seconds ticked by, but still the rot remained. Michael closed his eyes and redoubled his efforts, picturing the wood smooth and unblemished, sturdy and strong. When he opened his eyes, that's just how the wood was. He nodded, satisfied, although a little disturbed that it had taken so long. Still, it was fixed now. No, better than fixed. Never was.

He took the hoe down from where it hung on the wall, and marched back into the yard, ready to engage once more in the eternal struggle of man vs. plant. He stopped at the first weed he came to, a dandelion, positioned the hoe's rusty blade, and sliced into the earth.

On contact with the soil, the blade fell apart in reddish-brown bits and the handle snapped in Michael's hands, light and fragile like a kite frame. He let the pieces fall to the ground and stared at the flakes of rust that surrounded the unharmed dandelion.

From the porch, Sylvia called, "What happened?"

"Nothing," he replied, willing it to be so. But no matter how clearly he pictured it, the rusted metal fragments didn't coalesce, the handle segments didn't rejoin.

Lousy piece of crap. That'd teach him to shop at Builder's Paradise. He supposed he'd just have to do this the old-fashioned way. He knelt down and gripped the dandelion at the base of the stem and pulled. The plant should've come away in his hand easily, but it remained fixed in the earth, solid.

He tried again, with the same result. The dandelion would not come up.

He stood and regarded the weed, puzzled, and somewhere deep inside, more than a little afraid. He felt a bead of sweat trickle down his forehead, even though it wasn't that hot out, even though he hadn't been working that hard. He wiped the sweat away, brushed his hands on his jeans, and bent down once more. This was a dandelion; he had pulled up hundreds of them before without difficulty. This should be no different. He would make it no different. He gripped the weed with both hands this time, concentrated, and pulled. But if anything, the dandelion was even more firmly rooted in the ground than before.

Michael stood again. Screw it; he'd go get some weed killer tomorrow and zap the sonofabitch. Zap all the damn weeds in the yard. Funny, it almost seemed there more weeds now than when he'd first come outside. He probably just hadn't noticed them before. Yeah.

He picked up the remains of the hoe and started to head for the garage to throw them away, when a slim, middle-aged man came jogging down the sidewalk. Michael didn't know the man's name, but he was regular as clockwork, passing by the house the same time every evening, regardless of the weather—which is why you're out here now, a distant corner of Michael's mind whispered, but he paid it no attention. The jogger was dressed in a white T-shirt and blue shorts. He was tan and lean, and his muscles moved smooth and easy, as if oiled. He had to be nearly ten years older than Michael, but his graying hair still held a lot of black, and he had a youthful, almost boyish face.

The jogger noticed Michael watching him and waved. Michael gave him a howdy-good-neighbor smile and returned the wave. Then the man was past and, conscious of Sylvia still on the porch, Michael looked away.

"I guess that's enough yard work for one evening," he said a bit too loudly. He threw away the hoe, closed and locked the door to the garage, and stepped onto the porch to stand next to his wife and daughter.

Tammy was dozing, so Michael was careful to move quietly as he put his arm around Sylvia's waist and gave her a peck on the cheek. An inch from where his lips pressed against her skin, a tiny fissured opened. He willed it to go away, but it didn't. Fine, he'd just have to ignore it, then.

He gazed lovingly at his daughter's sleeping face, and if her hair was a trifle thinner than at supper, her ears now a bit lopsided, she was still beautiful in his eyes. A beautiful, normal baby.

Life was good.

They went inside as new weeds sprouted throughout the yard.

Michael struggled with Tara Jensen's bra clasp, trying to make his clumsy, alcohol-numbed fingers work. Tara's breath—redolent, like his, of Miller Hi Life—came hot and fast in his ear. She whispered his name, although it sounded a lot more like Jimmy, as in Jimmy Bedford, the boy who Tara had really wanted to take her to prom, but who had instead taken Cheryl Iserson, the girl with the biggest tits in school. Tara was intensely jealous of Cheryl, and had gone to prom with Michael to get back at Jimmy, who, Michael was certain, wouldn't care in the slightest.

Michael didn't blame Tara for being jealous. Jimmy was a star center on the basketball team, and quite handsome. He pushed the thought from his mind and renewed his efforts to free Tara's breasts, which were of a respectable size, if not in Cheryl Iserson's league.

Michael and Tara were parked alongside a deserted country road beneath an old oak. The windows of Michael's Nova were down and the air of a cool Spring night filled the car, although Michael was so hot and dizzy from the beer that he barely felt it.

Tara had been a friend of his since last year, when they shared a desk in art class. He knew her well, and when he discovered her disappointment and anger at Jimmy, he realized he could use it.

No, not use, never use. He wouldn't do that to a friend. He realized Tara and he could ... help each other out. He could take her to prom, so at least she'd get to go, even if it wasn't with Jimmy. And she could do what she was doing right now: help make him a man. For while he had dated a handful of girls throughout high school, even made out with some of them, he had never gone all the way. Hadn't been sure he could. But tonight he was going to prove it to himself, to Tara, who had joked on more than one occasion that he might not be ... normal. Prove it to the world.

If he could just get her goddamned bra off!

Tara pulled away and smiled, her eyes barely able to focus. "I'll do it." She reached behind her and with a single smooth motion, the clasp was undone. Michael felt like he had failed a small but important test. After all, weren't real men supposed to know how to get a girl's bra off?

Tara slipped the straps over her shoulders, baring her breasts. Michael could only see them dimly in the night-gray of the car's interior, their indistinct round curves, the dark splotches of her aureoles, the smudged dots of her nipples.

There they were; all he had to do was reach out and touch them, feel them, squeeze them. Do whatever he wanted with them. But the fact was that he didn't want to do anything with them. He felt no lust for the flesh offered before him, just embarrassment and shame.

He couldn't help himself, was too drunk to hold in the tears. As he sobbed, he hoped that Tara, his friend, would put her arms around him, hold him, whisper It's okay.

"Jesus, Michael." Her voice held no concern, no sympathy. Just disgust.

He knew exactly how she felt.

Later that evening, Tammy started fussing, as she usually did before bedtime. Michael scooped her off the threadbare blanket on the floor, where she had been playing with a tarnished pewter rattle before becoming instantly grouchy.

He left Sylvia to watch a sitcom rerun in the family room while he took Tammy into the sleep-conducive quiet of the living room. The blue paint was faded, the floorboards warped and cracked.

He made a half-hearted effort to imagine it not and wasn't surprised when it didn't work. He walked Tammy around in circles while softly singing "Twinkle, Twinkle, Little Star." She cried and thrashed at first, but within several minutes she had calmed and was curled up against his chest, eyes closed, head nodding. Michael enjoyed putting her down for the evening, did it almost every night. He liked being alone with her, just the two of them, in the stillness. And if she didn't feel quite as warm against his body as she normally did, he didn't worry about it.

He walked slowly down the hallway to her bedroom, not wishing to move too fast and jostle her awake. The globe of the hallway light was broken, the carpet worn and frayed. He walked into Tammy's bedroom. Normally the nightlight bathed the room in a soft, warm orange, but tonight it was emitting a sour green. Michael didn't allow it to concern him. At least it was enough to see by.

He laid Tammy gently on her side in the crib that this morning had been a cheery white but which was now black and worm-eaten, and as her tiny body came in contact with the now soiled, mildewed mattress, there was a soft, brittle snap. Suddenly fearful, Michael lifted Tammy back up, and in doing so saw what had happened, for while his baby girl was nestled against him, her right arm remained in the crib.

He focused his gaze on the arm and wished with all his might that it was back where it belonged. But it just sat there on the mattress, looking more like a plastic doll's arm than a human limb. For an instant he considered attempting to physically reattach the arm, but the thought that it might actually feel like plastic, might in fact be plastic, or worse, something less real than plastic, filled him with horror. And then, just like that, the feeling went away. Because everything was all right, everything was normal. It had to be.

He put Tammy down—extra-carefully this time—next to the doll arm (for that was the only way he could bring himself to think of it) and then covered her with a receiving blanket. She stirred, reached out with her remaining arm and drew the detached limb toward her mouth and started sucking on the fingers.

Michael felt his stomach lurch, and he turned away quickly and walked out of the room, telling himself that everything was all right, all right, all right.

He sat on the edge of his lumpy single bed, listening to the sound of violent retching coming from the other side of the cramped dorm room, watching his roommate's body shudder and convulse as he knelt bare-assed, emptying his guts into the waste basket.

Michael was twenty-two, a junior in college, although he still had at least a year and a half until he graduated. And for the last two years, he had roomed with Jerome Hudson. Jerome, who had been dating the same girl for the better part of those two years; Jerome, who had been talking about asking her to marry him; Jerome, who, tonight, had told Michael that he knew what he was. Who told Michael he was curious.

The taste of Jerome's penis was still strong in Michael's mouth. But Jerome hadn't come. Oh, no. After less than a minute, Mr. Curious had pushed Michael away and rushed over to the waste basket, vomit spewing forth before he was halfway there.

Dry heaves now, and between sobs, "Faggot ... fuckin' ... faggot!"

Michael felt like throwing up too.

After putting Tammy to bed, Michael sat on the couch in the family room and read for a bit, periodically brushing fallen flakes of ceiling paint off his book. Sylvia sat beside him and worked on a sampler as a present for a friend who'd just had a new baby. The fissure in her cheek was wider now, nearly a gash. And her left eyebrow sagged, as if the skin was coming loose.

Around ten thirty, Sylvia laid the sampler aside on the coffee table and said, "I think I'm going to get ready for bed." She gave him a meaningful look marred by her drooping eyebrow, and the bits of white paint floating down around her like ash. "Join me?"

Michael was weary from trying to ignore the changes around him, changes he was powerless to stop. But if he was to truly convince himself that everything was normal, that he was a normal man living a normal life with his normal family, then he had no choice, did he? He at least had to try.

He manufactured a smile. "Sure."

Michael nearly broke his foot on the way to the bedroom when a section of the hall floor gave way. But he extricated himself and continued as if nothing had happened. What else could he do? He couldn't make it not was, not anymore.

Sylvia was waiting for him, naked on the edge of the bed. The mattress, which they had bought new only a year ago, was now ancient and sagging, the blanket and sheets torn and full of holes as if a battalion of moths had been at them. Her thin, small-breasted body was criss-crossed with rents and tears, some only a fraction of an inch, some much larger. She smiled with the teeth that remained to her.

"Make love to me," she said.

He had never felt any real physical attraction for her, had always gotten through times like these with fantasies. Such as, for example, doing the jogger in the park when the man was only halfway through his run, sweaty, but still full of energy. But such imaginings were not going to help him get by tonight.

Still, he had his duty as a husband to perform.

"Lie back."

Sylvia grinned and a flap of skin peeled away from her neck. "What have you got in mind?"

Michael forced himself not to shudder. "You'll see."

She did as he asked, legs hanging over the edge of the bed. He knelt before her, steeled himself, and slowly, gently inserted his index finger into her vagina.

As he did, he felt something inside her break.

Sickened, he wanted to stop, but he knew he couldn't. His wife wanted him, and he wouldn't be any kind of a man if he at least didn't take care of her this way.

He started moving his finger in and out, slowly at first, then faster, faster. He concentrated on the sounds of the house as it creaked and groaned around them, hoping they would distract him from the terrible damage he was doing to her, but they didn't. By the time Sylvia's moans had risen to a squeal and her body shuddered with orgasm, her pelvis was a shattered wreck.

"Nnnnnnn, that wasss 'onderful." Her lower lip hung bloodlessly, attached by only a tiny shred of flesh, distorting her speech.

"I'm glad," Michael said, his voice quavering. "I, uh, need to use the bathroom." He turned and virtually fled the room.

"Huwwy 'ack, deaw!" Sylvia called after him. "It's youw tuwn next!"

He stood before the cracked mirror and gripped the sink to steady himself as tremors rocked the house, the porcelain crumbling beneath his fingers like chalk.

The house spasmed and suddenly lurched to the right. Tammy started crying, her voice wheezy. Michael wondered if her lungs were still working properly. Sylvia shrieked his name, "'ichael! 'ichael!" over and over, but her cries were soon lost amid the sounds of falling plaster and splintering wood.

I'll do better next time, he thought. *Just wait and see.*

And if next time didn't take, he'd try again. And again. Until he finally got it right.

His house collapsed upon him, but he didn't care. He was already too busy constructing the next.

COMMENTS

Here's the braided narrative technique again. I think it works well in this story, especially since the past scenes are realistic and the present scenes are surrealistic. Whenever you can provide your readers with a narrative structure or stylistic technique that keeps your audience off balance, that's great. Horror readers should never feel safe and secure with your fiction. They should feel that they're in the hands of a lunatic, and that anything could happen in the story at any time. Horror is about fear of the unknown, and a story's structure can help create that effect when it keeps readers as off-balance as the characters they read about. Once you start using one specific structure all the time, it can become too well known to your readers and lose its effect, which is one of the reasons I decided a while ago to avoid over-reliance on writing braided narratives.

I often try to build my stories from bits and pieces of my own experience, but it's not always *direct* experience. When I was a kid, I used to look at stolen *Playboy* and *Penthouse* magazines with friends, but I never had any trouble understanding why other boys found naked women exciting. And while I kissed girls in cars when I was a young man, I never had a traumatic experience like Michael did. I was comfortable giving those experiences to Michael, but altering them for his specific story. But there is one experience which wasn't mine that I used for a scene, one that happened to a friend, and I was *very* conflicted over using it.

I bet you can guess which one.

Yeah, the scene between Michael and his roommate.

The idea for this story was inspired by a friend of mine. I'm almost sixty as I write this, and when I was a kid, people weren't outwardly gay in my little southwestern Ohio town. Hell, I was a teenager before I realized my favorite cousin Karen and her "special friend" Sarah were lovers. In my town, any man who was sensitive, caring, and interested in things like books and writing (like me) was considered gay. For a time I wondered if the townsfolk might be right, and I experimented some, but one day I bought a book called *The Gay Mystique*. In his introduction, the author said he'd written the book for anyone who had questions about their sexual orientation. I read a few magazines such as *Christopher Street* before this, and the writers in them would often say things like "If you've ever imagined being gay, even once, then you are *definitely* gay." It seemed these authors were determined that readers identified themselves as gay, even if they might not be. But the author of *The Gay Mystique* seemed more accepting and less agenda-driven, and I felt welcome by his introduction. I moved on to Chapter One, and the author posed a simple question: *Have you ever been attracted to the same sex? If not, you're not gay.* I felt like the biggest idiot. I had never felt sexual attraction toward a man. In fact, during this time, I'd look at pictures of men in *Christopher Street*—no naked men, just ones in very small and very tight swim trunks—and try to see what other men (and straight women, for that matter) saw in them. I was like Michael with the porn magazine, except in my case I felt nothing for the image of a male figure. Was I attracted to women? Yeah, constantly, and I had been throughout my life. I stopped reading *The Gay Mystique* then, but I felt that I'd more than gotten my money's worth from the book. I should look up the author, see if he's active on social media, and thank him.

So I wasn't gay. But I started college as an acting major, and I was around theater people all the time, and many of them were out and proud, and my narrow horizons began to broaden fast. I became friends with a gay man around my age, and through him I learned about gay culture. (This was the 80's, the terrible days of AIDS.) My friend fell in love and moved in with his boyfriend and seemed very happy. But they broke up, and my friend—who also wanted to live what he grew up thinking was a normal life—decided to marry a woman who was a friend of his, so he could have a wife and kids, a house in the suburbs, a boring nine-to-five job, a new car, and a lawn to tend. Back then most people weren't aware of how fluid sexuality can be over the course of a person's life. Sure, we knew people were bisexual, but from what my friend told me, he had never been attracted to women. My friend told me that being in love wasn't that important in marriage. Being good friends and enjoying each other's company was what was really important. (And hey, my friend and his wife have been married for decades and have grown children, so who's to say he was wrong?)

Once my friend married his wife, he never spoke about having once lived a gay lifestyle again. I have no idea if he ever told his wife about his past, as she never mentioned it. It seemed to be a part of his life—and to a much lesser extent, part of mine—that simply faded into nonexistence. We've fallen out of touch over the years, although we're connected on social media in that nebulous way so many of us are these days.

Was my friend an unhappy gay man who entered into a heterosexual marriage in order to live what he viewed as a more normal (and in the AIDS era, safer) life? Or was he quite happy with his wife and the children they eventually had? I don't know. But the idea of someone who was determined to deny who he really was, even if he had to create his own fantasy world to maintain the illusion, fascinated me. So I started writing "Keeping It Together."

When I decided to use a braided narrative for the story, I thought about including my friend's experience with his roommate. It seemed absolutely perfect, but my friend didn't tell me about it so I'd have story material sometime down the road. He'd shared a deeply painful experience with me. How could I use it for story fodder? I felt like such a fucking vulture even contemplating it, picking at the metaphorical carcass of my friend's past. I didn't know what to do. Be true to my art and use the roommate experience or forget about it and maybe forget about writing the whole goddamned story. In the end I decided to use the experience (which you know since you read the story). I decided to do so because my friend didn't read horror fiction. He didn't read any fiction, really, was more of a nonfiction guy. I knew he would never see the story. I knew none of his family would ever see it, nor any of the people we hung out with when we were in college. One of the hard things about being a minor writer is knowing that only a few people in the world—virtually no one compared to the entire human race—will ever read your work, and even most of those who read the genre you write in won't read your stuff. But this is also a blessing, because it means you're free to include whatever you want in your fiction, since it's practically invisible. (This is why it's so important to find our own meaning and fulfillment in the writing we do, because most of us will receive little attention or accolades—let alone significant amounts of money—from the world at large.) So I felt confident that my friend would never know I used his experience in my story, and if anyone else ever asked me if that scene was based on a real-life event. I'd just claim I'd made it up. "That's why it's called fiction, dude." That's another wonderful aspect of writing fiction. Unless you tell people (as I'm doing in this book), they'll never know what's real in your stories and what's fabricated.

Still feeling a bit like a vulture, I started writing "Keeping It Together," and when I was just about to start on the roommate scene, the phone rang. It was my friend, calling to tell me his mother had died. We spoke for a while. Mostly I listened as he shared his grief with me. When the conversation was over, I hung up, sighed, and returned to my home office to continue writing the scene. In the end, I chose to follow my creative instincts, and I still wonder what, if anything, that says about me as a person.

I used aspects of my own life in the story. I was in my early thirties then, a new dad to an amazing little girl, so that worked itself into the story. I based Michael's house on my house at the time, and I really was outside one day when a jogger ran past on the sidewalk. I described him just as he was. Since I needed Michael to be outside when the jogger went by in the story, I decided to have him working on the lawn. I needed him to remain there for a while, so I gave him a supremely stubborn dandelion to wrestle with. The dandelion was a symptom of Michael's fragile illusion of reality, sure, but it was mostly there just to keep him in the yard.

I told you in my comments on "Mr. Punch" that I stopped going to writing groups after that story was published, and that's mostly true. A couple of us did try to form a new group. Gary A. Braunbeck lived in the same town, and I'd gotten to know him by this point, and Lucy Snyder had recently moved into the area, so we invited them to join. It was a good group, but we were all so busy with our writing that it was hard to find time to meet, so we eventually stopped meeting. I read "Keeping It Together" to the group, and everyone commented on that damn dandelion and how they saw it as an important symbol, one that stood for the story's entire theme. I didn't tell them I'd included the dandelion for a purely practical reason. Readers see elements in our work that may not be there, which is cool, but they can also draw our attention to things in our writing that we aren't aware we created until someone points them out to us—which is even cooler.

WHAT MIGHT I DO DIFFERENTLY TODAY?

Hoo boy. Where to start? I doubt I'd write this story today. Back then, I thought of it as a story about a person determined to live in denial, a person afraid of being their true self. The fact the character was a gay man was incidental to this idea. I chose to make the character gay because my friend was the inspiration for the story, and it's important to me to weave pieces of my life into my fiction. When I was an acting major, one of my professors taught us that the best way to invest a scene with emotional reality is to draw on experiences we had which were similar to what we were acting, specific times when we felt fear, joy, stress, etc.—whatever emotion the scene called for. This technique works well in my stories, and I use it all the time.

But even if Michael being gay had nothing to do with the story's concept and theme, how would readers know? They'd see the story as being a commentary about gay identity—or at least they'd be unable to separate Michael being gay from the theme. I'd learned a great deal from my friend about gay people and gay culture, but I wasn't gay and I didn't belong to that culture. I wasn't writing from my own lived experience. I'd appropriated a part of gay culture—coming to terms with one's sexual identity in a culture that doesn't always support that identity (to put it mildly). That's a story only a gay person can authentically tell.

Another reason is that, while being gay is perfectly normal to me, in a horror/dark fantasy story like this, readers might see me as portraying being gay as abnormal, sinister, deviant, even monstrous. Gays have been put forward as the Evil Other in so many horror stories and films over the years simply *because* they were gay, and I wouldn't want to perpetuate such a damaging trope in my fiction. So if I wouldn't write "Keeping It Together" now, why did I include it in this book?

So I could talk further about writing a story that deals with a specific identity when you don't have that identity yourself (as I discussed in my comments on "Huntress"). I also wanted to talk about the ethics of using others' experiences in our fiction. I don't have a clear-cut answer to give you on what's the right way to do it and what's the wrong way. Artists take in everything the world presents to us, it becomes part of us, and we draw on it for our creations. But I believe we should be aware of the material we're using, why we want to use it, and whether we should use it all.

One more thing about the gay-as-abnormal trope in horror. Not long ago I wrote a story called "Negative Space," which was published in *Nightmare Magazine*. It's about a man and wife who visit the wife's childhood friend. The friend has recently lost her husband, and she's doing her best to take care of her small children while dealing with her grief. Everything in that story is true—up to the point where the story becomes a surreal nightmare. My wife and I are the couple in the story, and we did visit her friend who was dealing with the loss of her husband. We spent almost a month there, doing our best to help however we could. There were three women in the house—my wife, her friend, and the family's au pair—and I often felt like I wasn't needed. Plus, I had no prior relationship with my wife's friend, so she naturally turned to my wife to process her feelings. One day, it occurred to me that I was witnessing the equivalent of a world that didn't need men, one in which men were absolutely super-fluous. For so long in American culture (throughout the world, really), men have positioned themselves as the center of the universe, and they don't react well to learning that they're really not as important as they think they are. I decided that would be the theme of the story, so I started writing. To further the theme, I had the wife and the friend become lovers as another symbol of the husband not being necessary. It never occurred to me that readers might view this as a statement from me that same-sex relationships were unnatural or evil. But at least one person saw the possibility that I was, intentionally or not, saying just that.

Nightmare presents an author spotlight each issue, and I was honored to be a spotlighted author in the issue where "Negative Space" appeared. Wendy Wagner is the editor of *Nightmare*, but Summer Fletcher was the one who interviewed me for the spotlight feature, and they presented me with some great questions. But I was surprised by one.

It's become something of a meme that men write women in terms of their bodies first and selves second (if at all), and I can see elements here that might be interpreted that way. Similarly, the narrator seems contemptuous of the deceased character for mistrusting queerness, but then presents his wife's moments of queerness as one of many surreal horrors. Do the sexual images point to distinct fears, or reiterate established ones? What would the ideal reader glean from those scenes?

My first thought was: "Oh my god, did I do all that without realizing it?" I was horrified, and I thought about my response for a long time. Here's what I said:

The story is about a self-absorbed man who feels that he's not only useless, but unnecessary, that maybe he never was necessary. Part of that is because he's aging, but a bigger part is due to male fragility. He believes he should be more important than he is because men are supposed to be important (or so his culture has taught him from birth). But neither of the women in the story need him, and neither do any of the children. The reason the women become sexually involved is to further demonstrate that he—and by extension, his entire gender—is unnecessary. I never intended for queerness itself to be viewed as a horror. The horror is the main character's redundancy as spouse, a man, a human being. That said, after rereading the story, I can see how someone might interpret the character's reaction to his wife and the widow forming a sexual relationship as a fear of queerness, and that could point to the character maybe not being so firm in his liberal beliefs—or his sexuality—as he thinks he is. Or perhaps it points again to the fragility of cishet men of a certain age who are confused and frightened as the world is changing around them.

Another way to show the main character's self-centeredness was to have him think of the two women in terms of their outward appearance first in the story. Part of that shallowness is because he's a stereotypical male-gaze kind of guy, but it's also because he has trouble seeing past people's surfaces in general—seeing what's behind the screen, you could say.

I was grateful for Summer's question because they got me thinking hard about why I used the story elements I did in "Negative Space." And everything I said in my answer was the truth as best I know it. But maybe on some level I'm unaware of, I am homophobic, at least to an extent. I find the idea ridiculous on the surface because of how many friends, family, and coworkers I have who are LGTBQ+. But saying "I can't be homophobic (or sexist or racist or ageist, etc.) because I have friends who are LGBTQ+ (or women or black or older/younger)" is always one of the bigot's first defenses. And as a white cishet male who's almost hit his sixth decade, I know I grew up with a privileged position in society, and that I'll be working to recognize this and fix it for the remainder of my life. I also know I'll never be able to get all the poison out before I die. But I'm determined to rid myself of as much of it as I can before I go.

For all the reasons I've discussed above, while "Keeping It Together" garnered little notice from readers and reviewers when it was first published, it's a story that looms large in my development as both a writer and a person, and it continues to do so.

EXERCISES

1. Look back at the previous stories you've written. Can you find any biases—conscious or unconscious, large or small—that may have crept into your work? If so, what would you do to address these biases if you were to rewrite your story? Be honest with yourself when you do this exercise. You don't have to share the results with anyone.

2. As I've said, I originally intended "Keeping It Together" to be about humans' ability—and sometimes manic desperation—to live in denial. We can be absolute geniuses at it. Using the theme of living in denial, see how many ideas for horror stories you can generate. If any of them seem compelling to you, write the story.

GHOST IN THE GRAVEYARD

Originally published in *All Hallows* (June 2000)

You approach the black wrought-iron gate that stretches between two squat red-brick structures that remind you of stunted turrets. The metal sign bolted to the brick of the turret on your left reads WEST BRANCH BURIAL GROUND. You've been coming to this place now and again since you were a child, over fifty years, and you wonder why you've never noticed this sign before.

You've only been outside the air-conditioned comfort of your Camry for a few seconds, and even though internally your body is still cool, your skin is beginning to react to the heavy, moist August heat. You feel a strange, almost numbing sensation as sweat begins to build, as if your nerve endings are in shock from the sudden transition from cool to hot as hell. You don't plan to be here long, you tell yourself. It shouldn't be so bad.

You reach out and grip one of the gate's bars. It's hot and slick in your hand and you realize that it's not metal you're touching, but rather black paint covering the metal. Something else you never noticed before.

You peer through the gate and see that the grounds are as well-kept as ever—the grass neatly trimmed, no broken tree limbs or leaves in sight. You have no idea who takes such good care of the place; you've never seen anyone working here. Perhaps, your imagination offers, the place looks after itself.

The gate isn't locked; as far as you know it never has been. You push your way inside easily, the gate moving smooth and silent, well made, well maintained, perhaps both. You step into the graveyard—or is it a cemetery? You always get the two con-fused. Burial ground, then. After all, that's what it said on the sign, right? You step into the burial ground and regard the rows of headstones. The markers are smaller than in more modern cemeteries, certainly smaller than in the one you just left. And while there may be less space between each stone, there's more between each row.

You don't want to look at the headstones, not yet, so you turn and look at the historical marker, set on a pole on the other side of the wall. You've never really read it before, only ever gave it a passing glance. You wonder why the marker faces inward instead of outward, so folks driving by might see it and be tempted to stop and take a look. Perhaps so they won't be tempted? Then why have a marker at all? You read, for the first time, the marker in its entirety.

West Branch Quaker Burial Ground. Erected 1948 in memory of Samuel and Anna Jay Jones. The wall contains brick from the Friends meeting house, which stood across the road in active service from 1804 to 1906.

You're surprised. A Quaker meeting house stood across the street? For a hundred and two years? You crane your neck so you can look around the sign. All that rests across the country road now are small, nondescript houses that wouldn't be out of place in any suburb. You wonder how you could live your entire childhood here, just down the road, and never know about the old meeting house. You wonder what happened in 1906 that spelled the church's end. Fire? Age? Or perhaps its members simply grew old and passed away, and their progeny moved else-where. You know of no other Quaker churches in the area.

You turn away from the sign, and look at the simple gray wooden building in the far left corner of the burial ground. You stride toward it, the summer heat finally starting to get to you. This isn't the proper atmosphere for a graveyard, you think. It should be overcast, gloomy, with a hint of a chill in the air. You wipe sweat from your forehead with the back of your hand, but there's too much and some drips on the lenses of your sun-glasses. You consider wiping the glasses off, but decide instead to remove them. You carry them in your right hand as you near the building, as if to underscore to yourself the fact that you don't intend to stay here long, otherwise you'd put them in your shirt pocket, right?

The trees—you're not sure what they are: oak? elm?—seem to droop in the heat, their leaves limp and dry. The treetops sway in a breeze that doesn't reach down this far. Or maybe there isn't a breeze and the trees are swaying all by themselves, your imagination whispers. You half expect to feel a tingle along your spine at the idea, as you would have when you were a child. But you feel nothing. From somewhere off in the distance comes the lazy thrum of cicadas.

You continue toward the building, careful to avoid stepping on any graves, not wishing to give someone in the past a shiver, you tell yourself jokingly. The building is a simple structure, four walls and a sloping roof, constructed from rough, weather-beaten logs. There are two windows, unadorned, no curtains, plain white-painted wood for frames. The left has a crack in one of its panes. All you can see through the glass is blackness, as if the building were filled with solid shadow. But you know it's just a trick of the light.

The wood of the featureless gray door is beginning to come apart in tiny threads, as if it were woven of some sort of strange cloth. Another historical marker here, this one affixed to the side of the building.

1804 Quaker Meeting House.

To commemorate the first church erected in Baker Township, Poss County, OH, this log replica was constructed in 1972 by the Baker Township 4-H Club and the Greenfield area campfire girls.

This sign you have read before. You read it aloud to your twin nephews the first time you brought them here, over twenty years ago. They couldn't have been more than four, and both were scared of going into the meeting house, so you went in first, to check for ghosts, you said. The boys looked at you, eyes wide with equal measures of fear and delight. And after you came out and pronounced "No ghosts," in a solemn voice, they repeated the phrase in awe and wonder. They walked around the rest of the day saying "No ghosts" to everyone they saw.

The boys graduated college a while back, and you don't get to see them that much, mostly just during special occasions, like today. They looked so grown up this morning, you barely recognized them. You know it's a cliché, but you still can't help wondering where the time got to. Maybe it came here, you think. After all, time has to go somewhere when it dies. Why not here?

You grip the rusty metal handle and shove open the door. It doesn't give easily, and you know it's been a long time since anyone's been in here. You step inside the meeting house—no, the replica—and find that despite the heat outside, the stale air in here is almost cool.

There's enough light filtering in from the windows to see by, not that there's much to look at. A half dozen crude benches made of split logs for seats and lengths of two-by-fours for legs. A lectern up front. The floor is covered with a scattering of dust, dirt and twigs. You look upward, half expecting to see a bat or two hanging from the crossbeams, but you don't. Just a small black paper wasps' nest, dry and fragile.

You wonder if anyone has actually ever used this meeting hall to hold a service, or if it's nothing more than a kind of graveyard tourist attraction. Perhaps the spirits who used to attend church across the street now come here to worship, or whatever it is the dead do. Or perhaps this isn't really a replica at all. Perhaps this is the hall from across the street. Perhaps this is where it came after it was no longer needed.

Your imagination again. This is just a project some 4-H kids thought up, or more likely some adult in charge of them. So what if the shadows huddled in the corners seem too thick, too dark? They're just shadows. You walk outside and pull the door closed behind you.

You step around to the side of the building, and there, next to the chain link fence that serves as a rear wall for the burial ground, is an old tree—an oak? And resting at the base of the tree, propped against the trunk, are three small headstones, their surfaces smooth and blurred by time and the elements, whatever legends they once contained lost forever. The stone is a bright green; moss, perhaps, or some sort of mildew.

You wonder why the headstones are here. Were they placed out of the way by whoever—or whatever, your imagination whispers—takes care of the burial ground? Did they fall naturally, or were they knocked over by kids? You and your friends never pushed over any of the stones during the times you played here. You always thought it was because your parents taught you it was wrong to vandalize property. Now you wonder if it wasn't simply because you were afraid.

Maybe, your imagination supplies, the bodies whose resting place the stones marked had gone to dust. And with no one to stand over, the stones fell, their purpose gone. Maybe the tree is some sort of marker itself, a monument to the headstones' decades, perhaps centuries, of watchful service.

And maybe it's just a tree. You move on, walking along the fence, not ready to look at the graves just yet. Less than two dozen feet from the meeting house, the grass gives way to a circle of bare earth. Another broken headstone lies face down in the circle, and you realize that it's been jammed into a hole, one big enough for a good-sized dog to go down. A groundhog hole, most likely. You've seen groundhogs in here before. One of your childhood friends, Eric Groves, used to say the groundhogs fed on the bodies buried here. You were always too smart to believe him, but every now and then you couldn't help wondering.

You ask yourself why didn't whoever it is that keeps the grass trimmed so neatly fill in the hole with dirt rather than block it with a headstone? The latter action seems completely out of character for someone who otherwise takes such good care of the place. Probably some kid's idea of a joke. You consider removing the stone and placing it over against the tree with the others, but you decide against it, telling yourself it's too damn hot.

You walk past the hole, thinking of the fun Eric Groves would have had making up stories about it to scare everyone. You wonder where Eric is now. Last you heard, he was a chemical engineer living in Texas. But that was years ago.

You think of all the things you and your friends used to do here. You would race weaving in and out among the gravestones, tell ghost stories to try to scare one another, and when it was dark—or rather dusk, for none of you would dare stay here once the sun was all the way down—you'd catch lightning bugs or, better yet, play ghost in the graveyard.

You're not even sure you can remember the rules of the game. It was some version of tag, except the person who was it was the ghost, and whenever the ghost touched someone, that kid had to fall down and lie still, eyes closed. The last person to be touched was the new ghost. Or something like that. It was really fun to play in full darkness, you recall, because it was harder to tag people, plus you ran the risk of tripping over the "dead" bodies. But playing in a real graveyard gave the game a special thrill that more than made up for playing at dusk.

At the time you used to wonder if the spirits in the graves you ran laughing and shouting over were angry at the disturbance. Now you think they probably miss it. You know you sure do.

Jesus, but you feel old.

You stop beneath a tree—an elm?—and wipe your forehead again, but all you do is smear sweat around. You gave up smoking when you were twenty-one, but you wish you had a cigarette now, even though smoking would probably just make you feel hotter. You wished you had a cigarette this morning, too, when you watched your father's coffin being lowered into a grave in a much larger and nicer cemetery on the other side of town. You tell yourself Dad's death was a blessing, that at least it freed him from the cancer. And even though you feel selfish for this—after all, it's your father you should be mourning—you can't help feeling that your childhood was buried along with him.

Your mother died six years ago of congestive heart failure, and now your father's gone too. You are officially and irrevocably an adult now. An aging adult with an ex-wife, no kids, and nothing really standing between you and the long descent into the same sort of hole that your father was planted in today.

Is that why you came here after the reception at your sister's place? To say good-bye to your childhood? Maybe.

You step out of the shade and walk toward the nearest row of gravestones. You begin reading names and dates. *John Hoover 1760-1813, Sarah Burkett (Beloved Wife and Mother) 1767-1843,*

Absalom Mast 1869-1908. Well, at least you stand a good chance of living longer than these folk. That's something to feel good about, isn't it?

You move on a few rows. The headstones here are smaller and made out of chalk-white stone. The legends are at once simpler and more ornate: *Wm. S. Pearson, died 1871, 5 Mon., 12 Day, Aged 37 Y.* Another row over and the faces of the stones are soft and blank, scoured by year after year of wind, rain and snow. You know just how they feel.

Despite the fact that you're wearing dress slacks, you lower yourself to the neatly trimmed grass and sit cross-legged on the hot ground, facing the blank stones. You wonder if some years hence—not as many as you'd like—your nephews will come here after your funeral to say good-bye to a piece of their childhood. You wish you'd made more time for them when they were young, done more things with them. But it's too late now.

As you sit and sweat, you fancy you see letters forming on the blank gray-white face of the stone in front of you, as if rising upward through murky water. Letters that form a familiar name. But it's just your imagination again. There are no letters, no name. Just featureless stone.

You stand, your knees protesting in a way they wouldn't have ten years ago. Time to leave. You've got a long drive back to the city, back to an empty condo and a boring job. Back to what passes for your life.

And as you start to go, you feel a cold breeze brush the back of your neck, its sigh a dry whisper in your ear which seems to say, *Tag, you're it.*

And the hell of it is, you know you are.

COMMENTS

I was thirty-six when I wrote this story, and as I've mentioned several times before, I'm in my late fifties now—basically the same age as the main character. It might seem strange that I, still a relatively young man at the time, was able to capture the feeling of being old and knowing Death is slowly approaching you. But my great uncle, whose name was Lawrence but who everyone called Red, died when I was nine. He was like a second father to me, and his death hit me hard. I fell into an existential crisis, wondering what the point of anything was if everything ended, realizing that time stole every moment of happiness the instant you felt it. How can humans find meaning in life when we're all so temporary? These themes have fueled my work for nearly fifty years now. In a sense, I suppose my early exposure to death caused me to age more rapidly than I would've otherwise, at least psychologically.

This story is really about the death of my mother, although it wasn't written until three years or so after she passed. She died at 59, the same age I'm going to be in a few months. So revisiting this story now feels strange, but also in a weird way appropriate. As I've told you before, my mother was a depressive agoraphobic who never got the mental health treatment she needed, and her death felt like such a waste to me, while at the same time coming as a relief. As much as I loved her, her depression affected the whole family, and when she was gone, it was like someone had opened a window in a sick house and let fresh air in. I used my experience with Uncle Red's death, as well as my mom's, and all the other deaths of family that happened between to fuel "Ghost and the Graveyard."

Everything in the story is real. The cemetery I describe is just down the road from the house I grew up in, and the gate is unlocked during the day. I went there a number of times to just walk around and look at the writing on the gravestones. I do have twin nephews, and I did take them to the cemetery when they were little. I did tell them "No ghosts." I almost used that as the title for the story. I changed details like the cemetery's name and the names on the headstones, but that's all I changed. I used the cemetery as the setting for another story of mine called "Bone Whispers" (which became the title of my third short story collection). I based that story on a gigantic groundhog I saw once when I rode my bike past the cemetery. The groundhog hole in this story was the one that big bastard lived in.

I originally wrote this story as a submission for an anthology called *Gothic Ghosts*, which was edited by horror legend Charles L. Grant and Wendy Webb. I knew Charlie from the old GEnie message boards, and I admired the hell out of his writing, so I was thrilled—and nervous—for him to read one of my stories. He passed on it, and in his rejection letter said, "This is a hell of a story, but I'm not sure this is the way to tell it." The snarky part of me thought, *What? You mean with words?* But even if Charlie hadn't spelled it out, I knew what he was talking about: my choice to write the story in second person.

Why did I use second person? It felt like the right voice for the story, simple as that. I have a vague memory of trying a draft in first and third-person point of views, but I'm not sure I actually did that. Sometimes if a story doesn't feel right after a couple paragraphs, I'll copy and paste it into a new document and change the voice and tense to see if it reads better, so I might've done this with "Ghost in the Graveyard." Some readers and editors *loathe* second-person stories, but I love them, and here's why.

Second person creates a distance between the main character and the reader. The unnamed narrator is a buffer between the character's consciousness and the reader's, and between the character's consciousness and itself. It's detached, somewhat cold and clinical, in some ways almost alien. Sometimes I feel like a detached observer dispassionately watching my own life, and second person captures this feeling perfectly. Many readers find second person unsettling, which makes it perfect for horror stories, especially more restrained ones that might fall more in the genre of weird fiction than strict horror. Even among people who like second-person narratives, the feeling is that they're hard to maintain over the course of a long story, so they work best for short fiction. I've never written a novella or novel in second person, but some day I hope to. I've pitched them to editors a couple times only to have them balk at the idea.

Another reason I love writing second person point of view stories is that the damn things flow out of me like water. I sometimes contemplate writing all my fiction in second person. I mean, if that's my most natural storytelling voice, shouldn't I use it more often? But as I've said before, I don't want to get into a rut of using the same kind of story structures over and over, so I hold second person in reserve and use it only when it seems absolutely needed. It's also another one of my writerly secret weapons. Because these stories pour right out of me, I know I can use second person whenever I need to write a story and the deadline's swiftly approaching. It's like second-person point of view is hung on my office wall behind glass that says BREAK IN A NARRATIVE EMERGENCY.

Since this story was a submission to a theme anthology, I wanted to find an approach that used the trope of a ghost differently than any other writers who submitted might. I wondered if I could write a story about ghosts without any actual ghosts in it, a story where the ghosts are memories and aging and feeling useless and unimportant. I often think of myself as a ghost haunting my own life—especially when it's late at night and everyone else is asleep—so that idea became part of this story's creative DNA. I knew I was taking a big chance writing a metafictional ghost story in second person, but that's the way the story turned out, and like "Mr. Punch," it felt *right*, so I submitted it as it was. Several years later, I met Charlie in person at the World Horror Convention where he accepted a Grandmaster Award. When I mentioned the story to him, he remembered it, and he was still uncertain about the point of view.

"Ghost in the Graveyard" is perhaps the most literary story I've ever written, and it would be as much at home in a literary journal as a horror magazine. It also works great for readings, especially if the audience aren't horror fans. In fact, I find second-person stories work great for reading aloud. Many writers advise reading first-person stories as it seems like a more natural voice for people to listen to. It's like they're hearing the narrator tell his/her/their story. I don't write that many first-person stories, so second-person is my substitute. I can feel an audience connecting with a second-person story when I read it aloud, more so than to third-person stories. I'm not sure why that is, but hey, anything that helps me connect with readers is a good thing.

"Ghost in the Graveyard" is one of my favorites of all the stories I've written. Maybe *the* favorite

EXERCISES

1. If you haven't written a story in second person before, take one of your previous stories and rework it as a second-person narrative. How did the change in voice change the story? Do you think it's more effective now? Less? Why?

2. If you don't have a previous story to work with (or don't wish to revisit an old story), pick a story from a writer you admire—one that isn't written in second person—and rewrite a couple paragraphs from the story, changing the perspective to second person. How did the change in voice affect the paragraphs?

3. If you dislike reading stories written in second person (or actively despise it), ask yourself why that is. Make a list of the reasons you dislike second person. Are there any items on the list that you could see as positive effects for a horror story? (Such as keeping readers off balance, creating a distancing effect, etc.) If so, pick one of those items and write a piece of flash fiction in second person to try to create that effect.

JOYLESS FORMS

Originally published in *All Too Surreal* (Prime Books 2002)

A decaying town filled with buildings of crumbling stone and brick, rusted metal, chipped and flaking paint. Cars up on blocks in the yards, dented mailboxes, wild tangles of weeds for lawns. The air hot, heavy, sour and raw. Breathing—if there were anyone here to breathe—would be like swallowing sawdust and glass shards.

On the edge of town like some gigantic tumescent mass lies the Factory.

A clump of buildings that looks as if it came into being through a process of slow, torturous accretion rather than planned construction. The exact shapes are difficult to determine for light draws away from the stone as if reluctant to touch it. Still, a few details can be ascertained. That the angles are askew is clear; that edges which should be sharp are instead rounded is plainly visible. Doorways are bricked over, window glass is broken or scorched and bubbled. Rusted barbed wire covers the walls and window ledges, clinging to the brick like thorny ivy.

The grounds surrounding the Factory are clear of any vegetation. Though whether the hard surface is soil or concrete is uncertain. If soil, it is earth from which the life has been leeched—perhaps stolen by the Factory itself in order to power its dark, enigmatic machines. Or maybe the life simply bled away, lost due to absolute and utter indifference. If concrete, then it is an uneven, sallow brand, its bumps and ridges resembling discolored brain tissue.

The barren grounds are ringed by black, spindly objects that jut upward like splintered, jagged fragments of obsidian bone. Trees, perhaps. But they seem too deliberately off-kilter, too consciously arranged to have grown naturally. But what else they might be but trees—and what ultimate purpose they might serve—is unknowable. So, for now, trees they are.

The Factory has been quiescent for some time. Days, weeks, perhaps even months. There are no clocks within its walls, no calendars. But look! A tendril of greasy gray smoke curls upward from a chimney shaped like rigid intestine. Once more there is work to be done.

Inside, deep within the Factory's twisting, shadow-choked bowels, workers who have lain dormant for far too long stir from their lethargy and begin gathering material. They move quickly, the dry husks of their insectile feet making *whssk-whssk-whssk* sounds as they scurry across saurian-hided floor. With skilled and practiced eyes, they search the corridors for only the best ingredients, harvesting bits of stale despair and impotent fury from shadow-drenched corners, prying scattered shreds of mean-spirited thoughts, shameful indulgences and debased desires off the ceiling.

To the vats, then, where these treasures are tossed into a thick primal soup. Batrachian creatures swim languidly within the vats, round and round, stirring, stirring. Finally, when the mixture is ready, faceless figures shuffle forth from the darkness, rusty buckets and mold-crusted ladles in their mannequin hands. When their receptacles are full of the viscous flesh-colored substance, the featureless ones file into the Shaping Room.

Here, deft serpent-fingered hands which may or may not be attached to arms—the light is especially poor in here and it is difficult to see—wait with barely restrained anticipation for the liquid to cool sufficiently. When it has, they begin working it, kneading, shaping ... Tiny arms and legs take form, smooth, soft, innocent. Round heads with a dusting of hair, small moist eyes, pink toothless gums.

The Faceless return then, and bear the nearly finished products into the Christening Room. Here, rotten-toothed mouths whisper into tiny shell ears, speaking in a guttural, inhuman tongue of the various dark destinies awaiting these newborns. The babes listen attentively, brows slightly furrowed, mouths sucking rhythmically. Despite their weak necks, occasionally they seem to nod.

Outside the Factory now. Long, reptilian trucks back up to the loading dock, their drivers—eyes too wide apart, ears set too low—sit silently, staring off into the distance without blinking while their trailers are filled.

Time to go.

The trucks pull out silently, save for a rough leathery sound of what aren't quite tires sliding across asphalt. The drivers have no delivery manifests, but then none are needed. They know where they are going.

When the last truck has gone, the Factory falls into hibernation once more. How long it shall slumber this time is uncertain, but sooner or later, it shall stir anew—when shadows grow thin and the world needs to be reminded of its truest nature.

COMMENTS

Can you tell I was reading a lot of Thomas Ligotti during the time I wrote this story?

Imitating other artists is a common way beginners learn, even if they aren't aware that, in a sense, what they're writing is fan fiction. As time goes on, their work becomes less imitative, they start putting more of themselves into it, and they start to find their own voice. And since genre fiction relies on shared tropes, it's always imitative to a degree. In that sense, we're all writing fan fiction of a sort, but fan fiction based on our having read many stories by many different authors instead of just one. Some writers never move past their imitative stage, continuing to produce work that clearly pays homage to Lovecraft, King, Barker, and others. If you find creative fulfillment in writing such stories and editors want to publish your work, then I see no problem with staying at this stage, especially if you develop your own voice. But such writers risk becoming a footnote in another writer's career, and they may never develop fiction that's wholly theirs and no one else's. Ramsey Campbell, Robert Bloch, and Brian Lumley all started out writing Lovecraftian fiction, and all went on to find their own voices and themes, although they occasionally returned to writing a Lovecraftian tale or two later in their careers. Ramsey still does from time to time. But Ramsey's an absolute genius and can do whatever the hell he wants.

But I was hardly a beginner by the time I wrote "Joyless Forms," so why I did I choose to write a Ligottiesque story? I did it to explore a different narrative style, one in which language, mood, and image were more important than character and plot. Neither of the latter appear in "Joyless Forms," unless you count the factory coming to life to produce a new shipment to send out into the world as a plot. Imitation can be an effective tool at any point in a writer's career.

I sometimes use stories as ways of trying out different techniques, too. For me, they're primarily learning exercises, but when you're a writer, you can submit your experiments for publication and see what happens. I'm a big believer in trying to get as much out of our creative efforts as we can. Unless an experiment is a complete disaster, why would I let it languish on my hard drive, when I can (hopefully) get it published, add another sale to my list of credits, and pick up a few dollars in the process? I sometimes use stories as prep work for something else I intend to write later. For example, years ago I wrote a tie-in novel called *A Shadow Over Heaven's Eye*, based on the White Wolf roleplaying game Exalted. Exalted is a fantasy setting based on Asian mythology with magic and martial arts action. As I was writing it, I got a contract to write a tie-in for Wizards of the Coast called *Thieves of Blood*, which would be set in their new Eberron game world. Some of the action scenes I wrote in *A Shadow Over Heaven's Eye* were designed so that I could practice similar scenes I knew I'd be writing in *Thieves of Blood*. Learn as you earn, right?

So what was I trying to learn by imitating Ligotti? I wanted to explore a different literary style that was more suggestive of its horrors than depicting them directly, and which hinted at much larger horrors behind the scenes. Cosmic horror expressed through the mundane. I wanted to try writing a story which left out one of the most important elements—character—and see what happened. Could I make the Factory a character?

I used a factory because Ligotti's stories often have manufactured creatures such as puppets in them, but also because I'd been thinking about writing a story about a factory for years. I'm fascinated by buildings I see when I drive along highways in the Midwest—old farmhouses and barns, houses in the middle of nowhere, and factories that look like they haven't been operational for years. I always wonder what dark secrets these places hold, and with "Joyless Forms," I got to find out. The title came from a poem, although I don't remember which one. I'll periodically go through books of poetry that I have, looking for phrases and images that might become titles. Often I'll rearrange and rework these phrases, then add them to the Titles file on my computer. When I need a title, I cruise through the list, looking for one that jumps out and says, "Pick me, pick me!" I may use several titles until I finally decide on one, but usually the first one I choose works, and I keep it.

Do I consider this a successful story?

In the sense that it did what I wanted it to do—experiment with a new style—yes. But as a story for other people to read? That's a more difficult question to answer. I never submitted "Joyless Forms" to an editor (at least, I have no memory of doing so). I included it as an original story in my first collection *All Too Surreal*. Would I submit it to a magazine today? Maybe. It's short, which is good. Editors can more easily find room in their magazines for short pieces. And it's a stylistic piece, which might make it a good contrast with other stories in a magazine. But it's a slight thing, and while I still like the grim undercurrent of the story, it doesn't make much of an impact overall, so I might put this into Save for When Someone Asks You for a Story and You Don't Have Anything Else to Send category.

WHAT MIGHT I DO DIFFERENTLY TODAY?

I doubt I'd write another imitative piece like this again, but who knows? If someday I read a writer with a really unique style and approach to horror, maybe I'll feel compelled to imitate them and see what I can learn. Because I've worked so hard so create my own style of horror—my brand, if you will—I'd be extremely cautious about submitting any work that might be too imitative of anyone else, especially if they were younger than I am. I'd look like an established pro stealing from a less-established writer, and I wouldn't want to give that impression.

But if I did want to submit "Joyless Forms" to an editor, I'd consider expanding it, maybe featuring one of the babies the factory sends into the world as a main character. What would it be like for such a baby to grow up? Who would raise it? What purpose is the child supposed to fill? I'd originally imagined that the Factory creates people who will spread darkness throughout the world, as if the Factory was where our serial killers, school shooters, fascistic politicians, and rapacious CEO's came from. Maybe my character would be a child who was faulty because he or she had empathy for others, and maybe the Factory would send someone—or something—to reclaim the defective merchandise and return it for repair or disposal. What would it be like for someone who thinks they're a normal human to find out they were manufactured in a factory? I might give my character a friend, family member, or lover who stands by their side throughout the story. Maybe this person would turn out to be one of the Factory's minions in the end. And if I wanted to, I could use the Factory as the basis for a novel. I've never thought about that before, but I can see the possibilities. Hmmmm ...

But it's quite possible that "Joyless Forms" can't be expanded beyond what it is, and that by trying to do so, I'd only make the story worse. Still, a *novel* about the Factory ...

EXERCISES

1. Try writing a story (or just a few paragraphs) that leaves out a core narrative element such as character, plot, setting, description, etc. How did it turn out? What was it like being forced to write without that element? Did you find it uncomfortable? Freeing? Did the writing turn out differently than what you usually produce? How so? If you only

wrote a few paragraphs, do you think you could expand them into a full story?

2. Pick a writer you admire who writes very differently than you do, then write a page or two where you consciously attempt to write in their style. Did you find this easy or difficult? Is there anything you learned from this attempt that you could use in your own writing? A different way to describe things, a different sentence rhythm, etc.?

BROKEN GLASS AND GASOLINE

Originally published in *Vivisections* (Catalyst Books 2003)

"There he goes again!"

Susan sat in the easy chair, the upper half of her body twisted around so she could look over her shoulder and out the window. It was dusk, but there was still more than enough light to see by. A car—painted a blue so dark it almost appeared black—came flying down their street, going well over the twenty mile per hour speed limit. It was doing forty, maybe forty-five, Susan guessed. She didn't recognize the make and model, but it was a sleek, sporty vehicle that looked something like a cross between a Camaro and a Jaguar. Whatever it was, she knew it didn't belong to anyone in her neighborhood. No one around there could afford a car that nice.

"Brian, hurry up or you'll miss it!" She didn't turn around to look at her husband, who was sitting on the couch watching soccer on ESPN 2. She didn't want to take her eyes off the car, almost as if she were afraid it might vanish if she did.

"Miss what?" Bored reflex, no real meaning behind the words. She doubted he'd even looked away from the pretty colors on the screen.

The sound of the car's engine grew louder, but it wasn't a regular engine sound—no rumbling, no hum of acceleration. It was more like the kind of sound fingernails made scratching on a chalkboard, or like the sharp point of a knife etching a line in glass. *Maybe it's one of those gas/electric hybrid cars,* she thought. She'd heard of them, though she'd never seen one. Whatever it was, it made a damn annoying sound. It set her teeth on edge and sent a cold wave rippling down her spine.

Then the car was in front of their house, flashing past in a blur of blue-black. She strained to make out the driver's features, but the windows must have been tinted, making the interior of the car appear to be filled with solid, dense shadow. She did see what looked like a face through the window in the rear passenger's side, though. Small, pale oval surrounded by darkness (a child's face?), hint of blonde hair, a suggestion of indistinct features— eyes, nose, mouth. Looking this way, looking right at Susan, locking gazes with her for a split second, perhaps even less as fast as the car was traveling, and then the blue-black vehicle was past their house, running the stop sign at the end of the street, turning left without signaling.

The sound of that weird engine hung in the air for a few seconds more—crawling deep into her ears like ants with sharp little feet—but soon it too died away.

"Did you hear me? I said, miss what?"

Now she did turn around, and sure enough, Brian was still facing the TV.

"That car," she said, trying to keep the irritation she felt out of her voice. "The one I've been telling you about."

A shaving cream commercial came on, breaking the mystic hold the television had on her husband's attention. He turned to look at her, frowning. "You mean the one that's been going through the neighborhood too fast?"

Houston, we have communication! "Yes. It just went by again, still going way too fast."

Brian made a noncommittal grunting noise and turned back to look at the TV. A beer commercial was on now, one that featured silicon-enhanced women in string bikinis.

"Brian, forget those bimbos. We're talking here." Despite her efforts, a strident tone crept into her voice. Cookie lifted her head, ears raised, and looked at Susan. The dachshund was curled up on a blanket next to the entertainment center where she'd been dozing, but the little dog was exquisitely sensitive to her owners' moods, and the tone in Susan's voice had alarmed her.

"It's all right, girl," she said in a soft, soothing voice, as if she were speaking to a child. "Everything's okay. Mommy and Daddy are just talking."

That took Brian's attention away from the boobs on the TV. "I really wish you wouldn't say things like that. I like Cookie just fine, but I'm not her daddy."

He barely tolerated the dog, but Susan didn't want to get into that right now. "I know you think I'm too worried about this car, but it's really a problem. Not only do we live on a narrow street, but people park their cars alongside the curb. A driver wouldn't be able to see a kid run out from behind one of those cars, especially if he was driving too fast. And kids play out in the street all the time, and people let their dogs and cats run loose. It's only a matter of time before an animal—or worse, a child—gets hit."

Brian let out a sigh that said, *I'm not going to get to watch the rest of the match, am I?* He picked up the remote off the coffee table and turned the TV off.

"Susie, I know car safety is a big thing with you, and that's perfectly understandable. But I don't know what you think we can do about this guy."

She hated it when he called her *Susie*; it made her feel patronized. Worse, Brian was a high school teacher—only a substitute teacher at the moment, but he was looking for a full-time position—and he had tendency to go into lecture mode whenever he wanted to make a point. Like now.

"A lot of people use our street as a short cut," he continued. "You can get off Frazier, go down our street, and get onto Smithville, avoiding three traffic lights and saving close to five minutes. Hell, we've done it before."

"Yeah, but we didn't tear down the street doing more than twice the speed limit."

Another sigh, this one saying, *Why am I bothering to argue? I know I'm not going to win.* In response, Cookie got off her blanket and trotted over to the couch. She jumped up, front paws on the cushion, and looked up hopefully at Brian, wagging her tail. His lips tightened in irritation, but he reached down and scratched the top of her head.

"All right, the guy's a jerk, I agree. But I'll say it again: I don't know what we can do about it."

Numbers flashed through Susan's mind. She was a bank teller, had always been good at math, had always found numbers reassuring, comforting, and solid. Something a person could get their hands on and really work with. She'd run across these numbers while surfing the Internet the previous night.

6,356,000 accidents. 3.2 million injuries. 41,821 killed. Car accident statistics for the previous year.

She wanted to offer them as evidence to Brian, to make him take her more seriously, but she knew what he'd think: that she was obsessing over this car, to the point where she was searching the Internet for accident information. And maybe he'd be right.

She made little kissy sounds to call Cookie over to her. The dog came happily, tail whipping back and forth through the air. Cookie rolled over and displayed her belly to Susan, who leaned down and rubbed it.

"I don't know what we can do. But we have to do *something*."

Brian looked at her, eyes full of love and pity, but that was even worse than his sighing.

She rubbed Cookie's belly harder. "Nevermind. It's just me. I'll get over it."

Brian opened his mouth as if he were going to say something, but then he closed it, nodded once, and turned the TV back on and lost himself once more in the soccer match.

Susan continued to rub the dog's belly, numbers swirling around in her mind. 6,356,000 ... 3.2 million ... 41,821 ...

Susan sat behind the wheel of their Honda Civic, concentrating on breathing evenly. It was dark out, but the porch light splashed the driveway with just enough illumination to see by. There were no street lights here. It was an older neighborhood, narrow road lined with small houses, most without garages. She'd thought it quaint when they first moved here, but she'd since come to view it as a lower middle-class dump—the kind of neighborhood where dirty-faced children played in the street, and unshaven men walked around shirtless, exposing snail-flesh beer bellies to the world. Where people hung out on the front porch drinking booze, playing music too loudly, and getting into shouting arguments. She couldn't wait to move.

Enough stalling, she told herself. *Let's go.*

The key was already in the ignition. She reached for it, noting with satisfaction that her hands were steady, and turned it. The engine came quietly to life.

Susan didn't like driving at night, and she especially didn't like backing out of their driveway, not when there weren't any streetlights. But they were out of so many things—milk, orange juice, bread—that a grocery run couldn't wait until tomorrow. Besides, her period had started a couple days early, and she needed tampons. She'd thought about asking Brian to go, but he'd landed a long-term gig subbing for a middle-school teacher on maternity leave, and he had papers to grade. So unless she wanted to bleed all over her clothes for the next twelve hours or so, she had to drive to the store whether it was night or not.

She pressed her foot on the brake, then shifted the car into reverse. But she didn't let off the brake. If Brian were here to see her hesitate, she knew what he'd say: *Why don't you just back into the driveway when you get home? That way you could pull out face-first when you leave again.*

And he'd be right, of course. That would be easier for her—*much* easier. But that was precisely why she didn't do it. She was determined not to give in to her fear, no matter what. So she pulled in forwards when she got home and backed out when she left, regardless of how difficult it was.

She gritted her teeth and slowly eased her foot off the brake. Their driveway sloped downward slightly, and the Civic began rolling backward. Her hands tightened on the steering wheel, and although the illumination from the porch light wasn't enough to tell for certain, she knew her knuckles were turning white.

Her mother telling her older brother to quit bouncing in the back seat. Her brother singing the lyrics to a song he'd learned in first grade music class. "I'm going to the zoo-zoo-zoo, how about you-you-you?" Her brother bouncing up and down in time with the song's rhythm. Susan giggling at her funny brother.

The Civic picked up speed, surely going no more than one or two miles per hour, but it felt to Susan as if the car were racing backward toward the street. She felt a surge of panic in her gut and she slammed her foot on the brake. Red light washed the driveway behind her as the car jerked to a halt.

Mother yelling at them both to be quiet so she could concentrate. Their station wagon backing into the street, the sound of a car horn blaring, Mother screaming, her brother screaming, Susan screaming too, though she isn't sure why. A jolt, as if a giant fist punches into the side of their car, the sound of crumpling metal, shattering glass, the world spinning round and around, and everyone still screaming, their voices merging into one sustained burst of pain and terror.

Then the world is still again and Susan—little four-year-old Susan—is the only one screaming anymore.

Susan's face and neck were slick with sweat. She could feel it running down her sides and back, trickling between her breasts ... Her breathing was rapid, and her heart felt like a small, frightened bird fluttering in her chest.

Get a grip, girl. That was twenty-four years ago. Just because some drunken bastard in a pick-up slammed into your mother's station wagon when she was backing out of the driveway doesn't mean it will happen to you.

Another thought whispered through her mind, a dark thought, and it was quickly followed by more. *Doesn't mean it won't, either. Doesn't mean anything, really, other than your mother and brother died and you didn't. If that sonofabitch had been coming from the opposite direction, they would've lived and you would've died. Your death would've been just as meaningless as theirs.*

And her survival? Was it ultimately just as meaningless? It was a question that had haunted her all her life, long before she'd gained the ability to articulate it to herself. It was a question that she doubted she'd ever have an answer for—wasn't sure she *wanted* answered.

"Fuck."

She took her foot part-way off the brake, closed her eyes, and let the car roll backward. When she felt the bump of the back wheels hitting the street, she opened her eyes and saw no head-lights coming from either direction. It looked like she was going to survive another night.

She let out a long sigh, finished backing into the street, put the car into drive, and headed for the grocery at precisely twenty miles an hour.

The next day after work, while Brian graded yet another set of papers, Susan went outside to prepare the flower beds in the front. It was mid-April, and it would be time to start planting soon. Cookie whined to come with her, and Susan put on the dog's harness and leash, and took her outside. She tied the end of the leash to an old tent stake and pushed it into the ground. Cookie gave Susan what she interpreted as a long-suffering look.

"Don't mope. You know you're not allowed to run around the front yard. What if you ran into the street and got ..." She trailed off, not wishing to complete the thought, almost as if by finishing it she risked making it come true. "Just be glad you're outside where you can watch what's going on and smell all sorts of interesting smells."

She turned and walked to the flower bed to the left of the porch and got to work removing dead flowers and weeds, dried leaves and other debris by hand, stuffing it all into a brown lawn waste bag. Occasionally, she glanced up, looking down the street in the direction the blue-black car always came from. It didn't come every day, but when it did, it was always about the same time. She checked her watch. Right about now, as a matter of fact.

It had been almost two months since she'd first seen the car roar down her street. It was February, and she had been out shoveling the driveway after a snowstorm. Only a few inches had been deposited and, given the forecast, there was a good chance it would melt off in the next couple days, but Susan figured she could use the exercise. Besides, she wanted to work off some steam. She and Brian had fought again last night over having children. Brian really wanted kids, but she wasn't so sure. They were both in their late twenties, so it was a good time biologically to start, but Brian hadn't found a full-time teaching job yet, and she only made so much as a bank teller. She wasn't certain they were financially ready. Brian said that there was no such thing as the perfect time to have a baby, and if she insisted on waiting for one, they'd never have any children.

There was another reason for Susan's reluctance, however, one that she wasn't comfortable sharing with her husband. She wasn't confident that she could bring a child into a world where you could be killed simply for backing out of your driveway. Her mother had been thirty-three when she died; her brother only seven. What guarantee would Susan have that her child would live to reach adulthood? None, of course. There never had been any guarantees in this world and there never would. Most people ignored this simple but cruel fact of existence and got on with their lives. Or, if they couldn't ignore it, they somehow found a way to make peace with it. Susan envied such people and wished she could be one of them. But she wasn't, and so despite Brian's desire to be, as he put it, "a *real* family," she didn't think she'd ever be able to have children.

So she shoveled snow, putting her back into it, trying to toss away a bit more of her anger and frustration with every shovelful she cast aside.

And that's when the car came for the first time. Moving way too fast, engine making that strange high-pitched scratchy noise, twin trails of slush splashing in its wake.

After seeing the car on a couple more occasions, Susan took to watching for it, and before long, she decided to do something about it. She called the police and complained, described the car to them, and demanded they step up patrols in her neighborhood. For several weeks, she did see police cars drive by more often, but of course, the car never came when the cops were around. She called and complained again, and this time a cruiser parked on her street for an entire afternoon, displaying a large SPEED LIMIT: 20 MPH sign next to another that said YOUR SPEED above a large liquid crystal readout. An officer stood with a radar gun, training it on every car that came by, their speed shown to all the world in large black numbers on a pale greenish background. Everyone slowed down as soon as they saw the cop, of course, but the blue-black car didn't make an appearance that day, either.

Susan had tried getting photos or video of the car to show the police, but it was moving so fast that they couldn't identify the make and model, let alone the license plate number. The last time she'd taken a photo to the police station, she didn't even get to speak to an officer, was asked instead to leave the picture with the receptionist, and she knew that she had become a nuisance as far as they were concerned, a crank to be humored and then ignored. That was the last time she bothered the police.

After that, she'd tried to get a petition going to have speed bumps put in the neighborhood, but she got very few signatures, and more than a few people told her in quite rude terms what they thought of the idea before closing their doors in her face. She had a grand total of six signatures when she finally gave up.

Now, out rooting around in the flower bed, she had a new plan. What she needed was the license plate number of the car—the police wouldn't be able to ignore *that*—and the only way to get it was to be outside when the car came by, to get close enough to see the number and write it down. She had a small notepad and pen in her back pocket. Now all she needed was—

She felt it before she heard it: a crawly feeling at the base of her skull that ran down her spine like a centipede with electric legs. Then the sound: fingernails on chalkboard, knife blade cutting glass, leathery tires rolling over asphalt.

Susan dropped a handful of desiccated leaves and stood up. Calmly, she began walking down the driveway, removing the notepad and pen from her back pocket. Cookie began barking, a high-pitched *yarf-yarf-yarf!* but she ignored it. She was trying to focus, to prepare her mind to see the license plate, to register the numbers so she could record them. The car was moving fast, and she knew she'd only have a few seconds to get the numbers down before it roared off.

She reached the end of the driveway, stopped, pen touching paper, ready to write.

The car approached, a bruise-colored blur with an impenetrably dark windshield. Susan wondered how anyone could see through that glass, it was tinted so dark. As the car drew closer, she had the impression that the glass wasn't tinted at all, that it was clear and what she saw were thick, black shadows roiling and seething inside. *Stop it,* she told herself. *Concentrate on getting those numbers.*

She trained her gaze on the front license plate, prepared to write, but then frowned. There were numbers there, she was sure of it, but they didn't ... look right. The figures were blood-red, and they seemed to swim in and out of focus. The harder she worked at seeing them, the more indistinct they became, almost as if they were changing shape as she watched.

Cookie's barking seemed to become louder, and it was accompanied by another sound now, the *whissk-whissk-whissk* of tiny paws moving through grass. She realized what had happened before turning to look: Cookie had pulled the stake up and was running this way, running toward the street ... toward the car.

She turned, dropping the notepad and pen as she did, and saw Cookie running pell-mell for the street, tongue lolling happily out one side of her mouth, the dog delighted to be free at last. Susan forgot the car, shouted, "Cookie, no!" and began running toward her pet. Cookie ignored her, of course, and put on a fresh burst of speed. The car kept coming, its strange engine noise filling the air, seeming to come from everywhere and nowhere all at once, like the rise and fall thrum of cicadas in summer.

Cookie was almost to the curb, and Susan knew in her gut that the dog was going to get hit by the car, crushed beneath its tires, little spine snapping, blood gushing out mouth and nose, intestines squeezed out her tiny rectum like coils of toothpaste from a tube. Cookie was too fast; Susan wasn't going to be able to catch her in time, so she lunged out with her right foot and stomped on the trailing end of the dog's leash.

The leash snapped taut and Cookie jerked to a stop with a gagging *arwp!* just on the other side of the curb.

The car roared by, tires less than half a foot away from the dog.

Susan looked up at the car, saw the pale oval of a face peering out at her from the back seat. It was definitely a little girl, no more than six, maybe less. Blonde hair, big eyes ... Those eyes moved from Susan to Cookie, any emotion they might have contained unreadable, and then the car was past and barreling toward the stop sign. As usual, it barely hesitated before sliding through the intersection and turning sharply, tires squealing as it drove off, leaving behind the acrid smell of gasoline and burnt exhaust.

Susan had noted that the car's rear license plate was no more readable than the front.

She bent down and picked up Cookie, who was shivering from the tip of her nose to the end of her tail and whining softly.

"Hush, girl. You're okay." She stroked the top of the dog's head. "Everything's all right." She stood there for a time, reassuring Cookie with soothing words, staring in the direction the car had gone, and knowing that she was lying to her pet. Everything was most definitely *not* all right. Not at all.

Yes, I think it's awful that Cookie was almost hit. But she wasn't, was she?

Susan sat behind the wheel of the Civic, engine idling.

And yes, it could *have been a kid instead of Cookie. But that's not what I'm most worried about.*

Brian was still at school. He'd had to stay late for parent-teacher conferences. Too bad; if he were here, he'd see that she'd finally taken his advice and backed into the driveway when she got home from work. She'd been sitting here ever since, car in park, engine still running, watching and waiting for over an hour now.

I think maybe you should see someone. You've become ... well, I suppose obsessed *is too strong a word, but ...*

After Cookie had nearly been run over by that asshole in the Bruisemobile, she'd gone inside and told Brian. She'd hoped that he'd finally understand why she was so concerned about this lunatic who insisted on using their street as a racecourse.

Maybe you could get a prescription for some pills ...

She didn't speak to him the rest of the evening, and she spent the night on the couch. What little sleep she got was far from restful.

The hell of it was, on one level, she not only understood why Brian was suggesting she seek counseling, she agreed with him. But it wasn't as if she hadn't seen her share of psychologists over the years. More than her share, beginning with the school psychologist in elementary school and ending with a doctor she'd stopped seeing a little more than a year ago. They all said the same thing in one form or another, variations on a single psychological theme: survivor guilt. Why had she lived when her mother and brother hadn't? If they hadn't deserved to die, then why had she deserved to live? If she hadn't been laughing at her older brother's antics, egging him on, their mother wouldn't have been yelling at them to settle down, and she wouldn't have been distracted. Maybe Mother would've seen the car coming, hit the brake before the station wagon backed out into the street. Maybe ...

It was Maybes like that which had been gnawing at her for more than two decades now. She knew there were no answers, no resolution, that she had to accept what had happened and get on with her life, that there wasn't anything else she *could* do. But no matter how hard she tried, she wasn't able to forget—wasn't able to forgive the four-year-old girl she'd once been for living.

She knew the blue-black car wasn't the pick-up that had smashed into her mother's station wagon so many years ago. But if she could stop it from barrel-assing through the neighborhood, prevent it from hurting anyone ... well, it might not completely cure her psychological problems, but she'd feel a damn sight better.

So here she was, lying in wait for the goddamned thing, intending to pull out and follow it until it stopped, whereupon she'd get out of her Civic and ream the driver a new asshole. *Then* she'd get the license plate number—and maybe even the driver's home address, too—and she'd give it to the cops and tell them if they still weren't going to do anything about the situation, they could shove it up their collective departmental ass. At least she would've done all she could.

Ten more minutes she waited. And then it came.

From the same direction as always, that teeth-jangling engine noise cutting through the air, windshield as dark and impenetrable as ever. But as the car neared Susan's property, she thought it slowed, just a little, as if the driver somehow knew what she was planning and wanted to make sure to give her enough time to get ready. Probably her imagination, she thought as she put the Civic in drive and pressed the gas pedal.

Blue-black flashed by—and that pale little girl face, too, hands pressed to the glass, looking straight at Susan with wide, wide eyes—as the Civic surged out of the driveway and into the street. She whipped the wheel around, tires squealing in protest, and tromped on the gas as her quarry continued on toward the stop sign at the end of the street. As always, the driver didn't slow, ran right past the sign and turned left.

Susan followed, suddenly realizing that if she had any hope of keeping up with the Bruisemobile, she was going to have to drive like it. Tendrils of panic brushed the inside of her stomach, and her hands gripped the steering wheel so tight, she wouldn't have been surprised if it snapped in two. Given her history, learning to drive in the first place had been hard as hell, but she'd been determined and kept at it, finally passing her driver's test at the age of nineteen. But in all the years since, she'd never gone so much as a single mile over the speed limit, had never merely paused at a stop sign before sliding through the intersection. Hell, she'd never even gotten a parking ticket!

But if she wanted to stop the blue-black car ...

She gritted her teeth, looked quickly both ways, and flew through the intersection, hanging a left as she did, tires protesting loudly. She expected to feel absolute terror as she continued in pursuit of the car, her speedometer hitting twenty-five, thirty, thirty-five ... but she didn't. Instead, she felt exhilarated ... felt *free*. She was surprised to find herself grinning as she drove, gaze fastened on the Bruisemobile's rear bumper, foot pressed firmly on the gas.

Street signs passed before her eyes, white letters on green: McKitrick, Peach Orchard, Bloomsdale, Harvey, a dozen others. Traffic signs were blurs of white on red, black on yellow: STOP, NO U-TURN, SLOW CHILDREN, SCHOOL ZONE ... Modest houses gave way to larger, more expensive homes, which in turn yielded to upscale businesses: doctors, lawyers, real estate agents, boutiques ... The blue-black car wove in and out of traffic as if the other cars on the road were standing still, and Susan kept pace, nearly colliding with other vehicles a half dozen times—horns blaring, middle fingers raised, faces contorted in anger—but still she drove on, one mile melting into the other, as if she traveled through a dream.

As night began to close in, Susan found herself trailing the Bruisemobile down the unfamiliar streets of a residential section she'd never been to before. A trick of the fading light made every-thing look distorted, as if she were viewing the world through rippling water. The trees were twisted, coiled things that jutted forth from the ground like splintered bone protruding from torn flesh. Shadows clung to their scaly bark like some sort of dark fungus. The surface of the street was hard, ridged and shiny, reminding Susan more of a beetle's shell than asphalt. The yards were devoid of grass, the bare earth gray and pebbly, resembling the rough hide of a lizard. She almost thought she could see the ground rise and fall, rise and fall, as if it were breathing. The houses were lopsided, patchwork conglomerations of building materials and architectural styles: brick, stone, metal, and wood, held together by red, raw strings of what looked like muscle and sinew; cape cod, ranch, Victorian, colonial, Tudor, two-story, split-level ...

Susan felt a cold numbness wash over her, and a thought drifted through her mind: *You've gone too far.* It almost made her laugh. Way *too* far.

Brake lights glowing a sour yellow-green, the blue-black car slowed, and then it turned and pulled into the driveway of one of the nightmarish houses. Susan no longer entertained fantasies of stopping, getting out and confronting the driver. She was no longer sure that there even *was* a driver. Wherever the hell she was, whatever the hell was going on, she only wanted one thing: to get back to normalcy and sanity. To get back home.

As she passed the house, she saw the Bruisemobile's doors open. A little girl climbed out of the back, and ... something else ... disgorged from the driver's seat. A mass of solid darkness that moved like roiling black fog.

Susan forced herself to look straight ahead and search for a place to turn around. She braked, whipped the Civic into the next driveway, tires juddering on its uneven, insectile surface. She stopped, threw the car into reverse, and hit the gas. The Civic curved back into the street, and she put it in drive and jammed the gas pedal to the floor. For a second—an awful, sickening second—the car hesitated, and Susan feared it was going to stall, but then it leapt forward, engine roaring.

It had gotten too dark to see and Susan flipped on her headlights. She screamed as they revealed the little girl, now standing in the middle of the street, looking at Susan with those big, big eyes and smiling.

The sound of the impact was softer than Susan expected, a soft thud that she felt more than heard. She slammed on the brakes, and the Civic skidded to a halt. She put the car in park, leaving it running, lights on, hot engine ticking. She opened her door, got out, nostrils recoiling from the smell of burning oil. She walked back to the girl who now lay against the curb, arms and legs sticking out in awkward, broken angles, looking as if she were nothing more than a rag doll tossed down by a bored child.

Out of the corner of her eye, Susan saw the shadowy mass that had been behind the wheel of the blue-black car begin to slide toward her, flowing down the driveway like a wall of solid darkness. She ignored it, knelt down at the girl's side. Got a good look at her face. It was a familiar face, though one Susan hadn't seen in a mirror for twenty-four years. It was the face of a four-year-old girl who had once lived when others died.

Susan picked up the girl, so small, so feather-light, and cradled her broken body in her lap. And as the darkness came for them, tears began to fall from Susan's eyes. Tears of sorrow, tears of guilt, but mostly, tears of relief.

COMMENTS

When I wrote this story, my family and I lived in a house with a very small front yard. Although it was a residential area, cars would sometimes go fast down our street, and—as an overly cautious dad—I feared my young daughters might end up getting hit by one of those cars. They wouldn't have to run out into the street. The yard was so small that if a car swerved just a little, it could jump the curb and plow into them. I don't know for certain, but I suspect a lot of horror writers imagine dark what-if scenarios like this, whether as a result of anxiety or—as I tell my wife—a healthy, realistic awareness of the endless malevolence of the universe. This particular dark what-if scenario became the seed for "Broken Glass and Gasoline."

Well, one of the seeds. The other was an image that had come to me some time before this of a parent kneeling in the middle of the street, cradling their dead child, as blood rained down from the sky. I have no memory of what might've inspired this image. I believe it popped into my head fully formed. It happens that way for me sometimes, and I don't question it. I'm just grateful for these gifts my subconscious sometimes gives me. While I was writing the story, the details of the image changed. Instead of it being a parent and child, I made it a person cradling the dead body of their younger self. And while I originally wrote it with a blood rain falling, I decided that was one surreal element too many, and it took the focus off the character, so I cut it. Whenever I think back on the story, I still picture the final image with blood rain, so maybe I should've left it in.

My short stories often have a psychological base, and the characters' inner worlds spill over into and merge with the outer, resulting in bizarre manifestations. I don't explain these manifestations because I believe explanations take away the power of these images. They just *are*. I think this approach works best in short fiction, though. For novels I tend to have more of an explanation—although not an overly detailed one—for the weird shit that occurs. When a magician's trick is explained, it becomes mundane. It becomes *known*. And magic (in both light and dark fantasy) works best when there's at least an element of the unknown to it. I tend to think of the kind of horror I write as nightmare horror, so my stories function by their own weird dream logic. Building up to a final, striking image can work well in a story. It gives you a direction to write toward, and everything in the story is designed to slowly create the image until the main character reaches what I call the confrontation point, the moment when they reach their terrible destination. This final image also results in what I call the suspended moment. The story ends with the main character trapped within the final image, so that image, and the emotions it evokes, are what linger in the reader's mind. The horror never ends.

One of the things I learned long ago as a creative writing teacher is that beginners will come up with a cool idea, and their story is merely a prelude to it. They save their best idea for last, and the preceding material often isn't very interesting. The technique can work if you make the whole story interesting for readers. This is why a lot of horror stories follow an investigation pattern or a quest pattern. Characters are presented with a mystery, and they need to figure out what the hell is going on, often in order to save their life or loved ones' lives. Giving a main character an obsession that plays into the story's theme—an obsession rooted in some event in the past—can give them a personal motivation for solving the mystery. That motivation can serve as the story's emotional core.

One of the exercises I sometimes do in my creative-writing classes is after students finish a story, I tell them to take the ending situation and make it the beginning of a brand-new story. The characters can be new ones or ones from the original can be used, with the plot picking up at the moment the previous story ends. This isn't a sequel, though. The previous story serves as background for the new story. After students write their new story, they're amazed to discover how little of their previous story was necessary to tell the new one. (Like I learned when I wrote the short-short version of "Daddy.") I tell students don't save your best idea for last. Start with your best idea and make the story even better as you go. I learned this approach from reading Clive Barker's "The Body Politic." In that story, Clive takes a well-known horror trope—the severed hand that gains a life of its own and seeks revenge—and takes it to an extreme. Whereas most severed-hand stories end with a character realizing *Oh, my god! The hand's alive!* and then getting choked, Clive's story starts with the premise that all hands have individual consciousness apart from us, and they're sick of being our slaves. They've been waiting for a messiah hand to come and lead them in a revolution against "the tyranny of the body," and one finally comes. This technique—beginning with a cool idea/image instead of ending with one—can create some wonderfully original takes on old, worn-out horror tropes.

Since I cut the blood rain from the ending of "Broken Glass and Gasoline," I decided to use it as the beginning of a new story, this one with different characters and a different premise. The result was "Long Way Home," which you can find later in this book.

The title "Broken Glass and Gasoline" comes from a lyric in a Bruce Springsteen song called "Highway 29." I don't remember being familiar with the song before I wrote the story. Most likely I did an Internet search for poems or lyrics associated with car accidents and "Highway 29" was one of the results. There isn't a wreck in the story, but the title seemed to fit well enough, so I used it.

The reason there's a dachshund in the story is because I grew up with dachshunds. They were my family's favorite dog, and—since they're the pinnacle of evolution on the planet Earth (at least, that's what *I* think)—I put them in stories every now and then. Dean Koontz uses golden retrievers, Jonathan Carroll uses bull terriers, I use dachshunds. In my two-volume *Shadow Watch* series, Bloodshedder is a dachshund by day and a huge, ferocious demon dog at night. At the time I wrote "Broken Glass and Gasoline," I didn't have any dogs. My first wife didn't like dogs, so we never had any. Years later, after my divorce and remarriage, my second wife and I got a couple dachshunds, and I realized how much I'd missed having these wonderful little dogs in my life. Both of those dogs are gone now, have been for over a year as I write this. My wife sometimes talks about getting another dachshund someday, but I don't know if I'm ready yet, or if I'll ever be. We had to put down our two small friends for different reasons only a few weeks apart, and it left a huge wound in my soul that may never heal. But since dachshunds are the highest life form on the planet, if we do get another, I'm sure it will use its magic to help me heal.

I often like to begin stories and scenes with dialogue. It puts the reader into a scene immediately, and there's character interaction going on, which means there's already a sense of forward story movement. Stories work best if they begin the moment when your main character's world changes, and while Susan has seen the car in her neighborhood before, this time when it drives by her house, her obsession about car accidents attaches to it, pulling her down a path she can't resist following. I recently read a Twitter post from an editor saying they're sick of seeing stories that begin with dialogue. I've never had an editor complain about this with any of my submissions, and I've never had a story rejected for this reason. Whenever I see posts like this on social media, I'm always afraid new writers will take them as writing commandments instead of a preference expressed by one individual. Like I tell my students, the only real rule in writing is you have to use written language to communicate ideas. Everything else is just custom, ways of doing things that most people in general agree on, but which aren't rules. So screw that editor's dislike of beginning with dialogue. If I want to start a story that way I will. So there.

When I reread this story, I thought about how I choose professions for my characters. I tend to avoid making them artists of any kind, although I will if it fits the plot or theme of a story. I like to give them common, everyday professions like teacher or accountant, as in this story. Sometimes I'll use an online profession generator so I avoid giving characters the same professions all the time. I try never to use horror writer or community-college English professor (my two professions) in stories unless there's a real good reason to do so. It seems lazy to me, and if readers are aware these are my jobs (and they will be from my story bio), I think it pulls them out of the world of the story by reminding them too much of the real world. But hey, Stephen King makes his characters writers or teachers all the time, and it works for him.

I said earlier that what I remember most about this story is the original final image that was the inspiration for it. Like most of the stories in this book—the older ones especially—I didn't recall much detail before rereading them. When I first started going to cons and listening to writers speak on panels, I always found it mystifying when writers would claim not to remember much about their older work. *How could they ever forget writing a story?* I thought. Fast forward a few decades later, and I now know those writers were telling the truth. Not only can't I remember details about my stories, I may not remember anything about them, even ones I wrote only a few months ago. People might tell me they liked a certain story of mine they read in an anthology, and I'll thank them for telling me and say I'm glad they enjoyed it (and I am!), but I have absolutely no idea what the story is about, not even the merest scrap of memory about premise, plot, or character. This isn't true for everything I write, of course, but it happens more often than it used to. I fear it may be a sign of aging. My wife says it's because I've got so much going on in my head all the time and because I'm prolific, always moving from one project to the next. I like her explanation better.

WHAT MIGHT I DO DIFFERENTLY TODAY?

I think I would put the blood rain back in at the end and see if I thought the climax works better that way. Instead of doing a braided narrative for this story, alternating between present and past scenes, I had fragments of memory intrude into Susan's thoughts during present scenes. That can be a good technique to show the past haunting a character's thoughts without clogging up your story with excess past scenes it may not need. I like the way I used that technique in this story, but I might play around with making it a truly braided narrative and see how that works. I'd probably try to come up with a different title since there's no car wreck in the story. Toward the end, Susan enters a distorted version of our world. I've used this kind of thing in other stories and in novels, often described the same way. I might cut that element or at least come up with different descriptions for it. I'm not sure the story events set up the final image well enough. Whenever I write stories like this, I never know how much set up and explanation is necessary and how much is too much, so I end up depending on editors to tell me. If they want me to make things a little clearer, I'm happy to do so. That works for when I've been invited to submit a story for an anthology or magazine.

If I write a story first and submit it unsolicited to an editor, not explaining enough can be a reason for a rejection, and editors are usually too busy to give you feedback on why they didn't accept your story. As author Tom Piccirilli once said in his book *Welcome to Hell: A Guide for the Beginning Writer* (and I paraphrase), *it's not an editor's job to teach you how to be a better writer; it's their job to find stories to put in their magazines.* It may take a while for unsolicited stories I write to find a home, but that's okay. It's all part of the deal.

EXERCISES

1. Do an image search on Google using key words like *bizarre, surreal, dream, nightmare,* etc. If you like, add words like *picture, art,* or *image* after these words. You'll find a lot of cool, weird stuff. Pick an image that appeals to you, and write a story that builds up to that image in the end and see what you come up with. If you like your story and want to publish it, change the image somewhat so it's not an exact replica of the image that inspired it. One of my college professors shared an old writers' joke with the class— *Good writers borrow; great writers steal.* But you don't want to get accused of plagiarism, do you?

2. Write a scene using the fragmentary memory technique I used in "Broken Glass and Gasoline," or return to a previously written story of yours and add in some intrusive fragmentary memories that hint at a character's past. Did you like the technique? What advantages does it have that the fully-developed flashbacks don't? What advantages do flashbacks have that fragmentary memories don't?

WATERS DARK AND DEEP

Originally published in *Masques V* (Gauntlet Press 2006)

Water roaring in her ears, pushing heavy against her ear drums. Hands clawing for purchase, feet kicking, trying to find something, anything solid to stand on, but there's nothing—nothing but water. She opens her mouth to scream, takes a deep breath first, but instead of filling her lungs with air, liquid rushes down her throat and a shower of bubbles bursts from her mouth. Her lungs feel full and heavy, as if they're filled with concrete and it's weighing her down, down, down ...

My camera! she thinks. I can't lose my camera? Mom and Dad will kill me!

She looks up, sees a scattered diffusion of light somewhere above her—five feet? Five hundred? There's no real difference at this point. There's a whole world of air up there, if only she could reach it. If only she was wearing a life jacket, if only she had learned how to swim ...

A small shape slides toward her through the gray murk: sleek, scaled and streamlined. It's a fish of some sort. Daddy would know what kind, but she doesn't. It turns as it nears her face, displaying its flank, a cold black eye looking at her with supreme indifference as it passes, and then it's gone, returned once more to the darkness it came from, and she's still going down, down, down ...

"It's all right? You're all right!"

Tina struggled to catch her breath. She was sitting up in bed, covered in sweat, chest heaving. Carl sat next to her, hands firm on her bare shoulders as if he were trying to hold her down. The bedroom was dark; it was still night. The darkness made her think of her dream—of the water—and she shivered.

"Light," she managed to gasp out. "Please ... turn on the light."

Carl removed a hand from her shoulder and leaned over to switch on the night stand lamp. Soft yellow light illuminated her small apartment bedroom, but the corners remained dim and shadowy. *Murky,* she thought. *Like water.*

Carl began kneading her shoulders. "You had a bad dream."

Tina's pulse was racing, and she felt as if she couldn't catch her breath, but she still managed a soft chuckle. "No kidding."

They were both naked; normally she slept in a nightgown, but not when Carl stayed over. The sheet was thrown back, the blankets twisted into knots. She must've thrashed around quite a bit before Carl woke her. Without thinking about it, she leaned forward and began straightening the covers.

"Same one?" Carl asked.

She nodded. "That's the third time I've had it this week. I don't know why. I mean, I used to have it a lot when I was kid, but I haven't had it for *ages.*" She paused, checked the sheets and covers, gave them one last smoothing with her palm. There.

"Until now," Carl added.

"Yes." She turned toward him and forced a smile. It wasn't hard to do. He was a boyishly handsome man who kept himself trim by working out and doing a little bodybuilding. Maybe he was no Mr. Universe, but he sure looked good with his clothes off. Besides, she loved him like crazy, which was a good thing considering that they were engaged to be married.

"Maybe it's just stress. You've got a lot going on in your life: your job, getting ready to start on your MBA ..."

She smiled. "And don't forget our impending nuptials."

A flicker of something passed across his face, a hint of an expression that was gone before it could be fully born. It was his turn to smile then, but it was a thin smile, one that hardly counted as a smile at all, really.

A second passed, then another, before he answered. "Right." The word seemed toneless and devoid of meaning, like it had been emitted from a computer speaker rather than the mouth of a man she intended to marry.

She wondered if something were wrong, if she should ask him if everything was okay, but then she glanced at the digital clock on the nightstand and saw that it was sixteen minutes after four in the morning. He was probably just tired and out of sorts from being woken by her thrashing about. That's all.

She snuggled into his arms and they lay back on the bed, holding each other.

"You know what I say about stress."

He sighed, smiled. "'Pressure makes diamonds.' I think you've attended one too many corporate training seminars."

She ignored the dig. "It's all a matter of whether you let things get to you or not. Anything can be controlled—including stress—if you work at it hard enough."

"It's a good life if you don't weaken, eh?" He kept one arm around her as he rolled halfway over and reached for the lamp.

"Carl? Could you ... leave it on? Just for a little bit, until I fall asleep?"

He hesitated, but then said, "Sure," and rolled back over to kiss her. It wasn't a quick kiss, but it wasn't exactly a lingering one, either. "Night." He disengaged from her and turned over on his side, his back to her. She felt hurt, even though he slept like that a lot of the time. But after the nightmare she'd had, she could've used a little extra TLC.

Her lips were still moist with his saliva, and it felt ... funny, thicker than it should, cooler. She touched fingers to her lips, brought them to her nose, sniffed—

—and smelled the faint, brackish odor of lake water.

Tina hoped she wasn't sweating too badly. It was late June, and in southwestern Ohio, that meant high humidity. She could feel moisture being sucked out of her pores with every clack of her high-heel shoes, and she wished she hadn't worn her blue blazer and skirt today. The fabric was *way* too heavy for summer, but it was the nicest outfit she had, and she wanted to make a good impression on the doctors at this practice. Maybe free samples were what really sold pharmaceuticals—and her case was bulging full of those today—but looking good in the bargain sure didn't hurt. *Especially* when the practice was staffed by all male doctors, like this one.

As a pharmaceutical sales rep, she was always careful not to park too close to the entrance of a physician's office. Docs hated it when you took up spaces they thought should be reserved for their patients. Ordinarily, it wasn't much of a hassle, but the office park was crowded today, and she'd been forced to park her Geo Metro in front of an orthodontist's the equivalent of a city block away. The way she was sweating, by the time she got inside, she'd be lucky if she didn't look like a drowned rat.

She remembered the dream she'd had last night, and despite the heat of the day, she felt a chill ripple along her spine. Maybe *drowned* rat wasn't the best choice of image for a simile.

Tina heard a soft *squeeek-squeeek-squeeek* of turning wheels. She turned toward the sound and saw a small woman—*really* small, so tiny she looked more like an ambulatory doll than a creature of flesh and blood—pushing herself across the parking lot on a stainless steel scooter. Tina wondered if there were something wrong with the woman's legs, if they were too weak to support even her minimal weight and she needed the scooter to get around.

The woman had blonde hair down to the center of a tiny back, and she wore a white dress and shoes that were so small they looked like they belonged on a doll rather than a person. The woman's head was out of proportion with her body, so much so that it seemed she might topple over any moment, her head dragging the rest of her body down to the blacktop of the parking lot. She was so small, so thin that Tina imagined she wouldn't make much of a sound when she hit, no more than a child's stuffed animal dropped onto carpet. The little woman held onto the handlebars with stubby sausage-link fingers as she half-walked, half-scooted toward Tina, wheels *squeeeeeeking* softly.

Tina felt the flesh on the back of her neck crawl as the woman approached, and she almost turned around and hurried back to her car. But she stood her ground, afraid of hurting the woman's feelings and, more to the point, blowing her sales call. Besides, if Tina avoided contact with the woman because of her appearance, that would make her a ... what? Not a racist. A height-ist? Something like that.

As the woman drew near, Tina relied on her years of sales experience to conceal her true feelings. *Just act like you're talking to a customer.* She took a breath, released it, forced her body to relax and put on a "you don't know me yet, but we're destined to be good friends" smile.

The little woman reached the sidewalk, stood and half-lifted, half-walked her bike onto it, sat back down, and then rolled right up to Tina, the front wheel of her scooter bumping into Tina's left shoe. Tina didn't wait for the woman to speak; in sales, it was vital to get the first word in yourself.

"Hi." Opening lines flashed nervously through her mind and were discarded just as quickly as they came. *Nice day for a bike ride ... Doing a "little" shopping? ... How's the weather down there? ...*

But whatever Tina might've said died unspoken when she took a good look at the woman's face. Her skin was pale, almost grayish-white, her lips round, the flesh puckered and tight as if they didn't belong to a mouth at all but an entirely different orifice. Worst of all, though, were the little woman's eyes. They were large, moist and black, like ebon marbles with petroleum jelly smeared on the surfaces. Tina had the impression that she'd seen these eyes before, but she couldn't ...

And then she remembered. They resembled the eyes of the fish that had swam past her face when she'd almost drowned as a kid. These eyes had the same cold alien quality: detached, distant, and utterly devoid of any shred of human emotion.

The orifice that served at the woman's mouth irised open and she spoke, her voice liquid and phlegmy. "In the end, control is a fragile illusion. The more you struggle to hold onto it, the more easily it shatters in your grasp." Her mouth opened and closed once, twice more without making any sound, as if she were gawping for air. She scooted backwards a foot, turned the front wheel of her tiny bike, and then advanced, making her way around Tina, wheels *squeak-squeak-squeaking.*

Tina turned to watch the little woman continue down the sidewalk away from her. The woman's cryptic words swirled around in her mind, but they weren't what bothered Tina the most. What truly disturbed her was the glimpse she'd gotten of the little woman's hands as she'd pulled her bike back and then moved forward. She'd seen that those stubby fingers were connected by gossamer-thin webs of skin—skin covered with glistening scales.

She felt dizzy, nauseated, and then Carl's words from last night returned to her.

Maybe it's just stress. You've got a lot going on in your life: your job, getting ready to start your MBA ... Not to mention the wedding, which Carl hadn't. But maybe he was right. She *was* under a great deal of stress, more than she ever had been before. So she had encountered a strange little woman on her way to a sales call—what of it?

What about those eyes ... those fingers?

Stress could do funny things to a person's perceptions. The little woman on the bike had been real enough, and she'd said those words, whatever the hell they were supposed to mean, but the eyes and the webbed fingers? Uh-uh. Not a chance they were real. A trick of the light, the mind, or both. Best to just forget about them and move on.

She continued down the sidewalk, passing office fronts—real estate, financial planning, an optometrist's—on her way to the doctors'. The encounter with the little woman might have shaken her a bit, but at least it hadn't put her behind schedule.

She was mentally rehearsing her opening spiel for whichever doc might be available to see her (and trying to decide if it would be too obvious if she undid another button on her blouse), when she felt a tightness in her chest. It wasn't much at first, just a sensation as if she were wearing constricting clothes, but then it worsened, and her lungs began to feel heavy, as if they were filling with fluid. Breathing became more difficult, until it felt as if she were trying to suck air through a mouthful of wet cotton. Her pulse rate soared, and she could feel her heart pounding in her ears, the sound not unlike the rushing gurgle of water.

Panic surged through her. She dropped her sample case and ran toward the doctors' office, high-heels clack-clack-clacking on the sidewalk as she wheezed and gasped for air. Her vision began to go gray around the edges (a gray that resembled the murkiness of silty lake water) and she prayed that she'd reach the office doors before she lost consciousness.

Almost there, almost—

Tina drove away from the doctor's, embarrassed and angry at herself. She was a professional woman, goddamnit, not some simpering little thing that let her "nerves" get to her.

I suggest you make an appointment with your regular doctor to see if he or she would like to run some more tests, but based on my examination, I'd say you experienced a mild panic attack, brought on most likely by stress. Not a lot of fun, of course, but nothing serious.

The doctor had smiled then—a patronizing smile, Tina thought, one that said: "There's nothing wrong with you, so leave now and let me get on with seeing patients who *really* need me."

He'd also offered to write her a short-term prescription for anti-anxiety medication until she could get in to see her regular doctor, but she'd declined. She hated the idea of taking pills to alter her emotions. They were *her* emotions, and if they needed to be controlled, then she would be the one to do it, not some damn medicine. Not exactly an attitude her supervisor at Pharm-Tech would approve of, maybe, but that's how she felt.

The words the little woman (the little *fish* woman, she couldn't help thinking) had said came back to her then.

In the end, control is a fragile illusion. The more you struggle to hold onto it, the more easily it shatters in your grasp.

"Bullshit," she whispered, but without much conviction. She continued driving toward her next sales call and tried not to think about the little woman's cold, black eyes. Tried very hard.

When Tina was twelve, she almost drowned.

Her family had been vacationing at a state park that summer: her father, mother, little brother and herself, all crammed into a tiny tin can of a trailer for a week. She'd never been the out-doorsy type and was well and truly bored after the first couple days. Besides, there really wasn't that much to do, not with her parents. Her dad liked to go fishing, but her mom was too afraid to get into the boat—she was worried about tipping over, about getting sunburned, about getting eaten alive by mosquitoes—so she remained at the trailer, staying inside and reading or watching the portable TV they'd brought, even though they could only pick up two local channels out of Cincinnati. Her brother liked to fish, too, so he accompanied their father, which left Tina (who *loathed* fishing) with only two choices: stay at the trailer with Mom or roam around the park and see what trouble she could get into.

And on the last day of their vacation, Tina found trouble all right. Found plenty.

She wandered down to the boat dock, hoping to see the cute guy who worked at the nearby food stand. He was a teenager—sixteen, maybe seventeen—and, at least in Tina's eyes, he was movie-star handsome. She had no illusions that the boy would fall in love with her. At twelve she was coltish and awkward, and besides, her family was leaving for home later. But she just wanted to see him one last time, and maybe, if she was lucky, snap a picture of him with the camera Aunt Karen had given her for her last birthday.

But—rotten luck—the boy hadn't been working that day, so bored *and* depressed now, she walked to the end of the dock, thinking maybe she might see a crane or something flying over the water and get a picture of it.

Her mother would've had a fit if she'd seen, because Tina had never learned how to swim and, despite Mom's advice, she wasn't wearing a lifejacket. There was no *way* Tina was going to wear one of those bulky orange things. Not only would she look like a big geek since all she was doing was walking on the dock, they were itchy and uncomfortably hot. She wasn't stupid; she'd be careful not to get too close to the water. And even if she did fall in, she'd be so close to the dock that she could pull herself out easily.

So she stood at the end of the dock, sandals hanging over the edge by a half inch, and she looked down and saw a school of small darting fish in the water. They weren't exactly a crane, but she figured they'd do. She brought the camera (which was hanging by a black strap around her neck) up to her eye and gazed through the lens, struggling to focus it. She wasn't sure if she'd be able to get the picture—would the camera be able to shoot something that was under the water? Maybe if she leaned down a little ... a bit more ... just a—

And then the world swayed, tilted, and she was in the water.

She went down once, twice, and was about to go down for the third time when she felt a strong, sure hand close around her wrist and pull her up. *Let it be him,* she thought, hoping that the cute food-stand boy would turn out to be her savior. But it wasn't. She was saved by a fat little man with bad skin and a sunburned bald head. Still, she wasn't too disappointed. She was alive, after all, though her camera was completely ruined.

Her T-shirt and shorts were still sopping wet by the time she got back to the trailer, and her mother nearly had a heart attack when Tina explained what had happened.

She hugged Tina so tight she could barely breathe and said, "I'll never take you to such a dangerous place again!"

And she was true to her word. Tina's family never went on vacation after that, not even a simple day trip. Before long her mother didn't want to go anywhere, for any reason. By the time she died of congestive heart failure when Tina was twenty-five, her mom hadn't left the house for over a decade.

Tina had been terrified by the experience of nearly drowning. The complete and total loss of control—not being able to breathe, unable to stop herself from sinking—had shaken her to the core. But when she saw how her mother reacted to the incident, Tina decided that she wouldn't let it get to her, wouldn't let her fear make her retreat from the world. She took a paper route, saved her money, and signed up for swimming lessons at the Y. By the time she entered high school, she was good enough to be on the swim team, and by the time she graduated, she was able to go to college on a partial swimming scholarship.

Tina first heard the phrase "pressure makes diamonds" from her swimming coach in high school, and she liked it so much she decided to make it her personal motto. Whatever happened to her, no matter how bad it was, she would handle it. She'd taken control of her life, and she was never going to let it get out of her control again.

"C'mon, c'mon ..." Tina urged the driver ahead of her to go faster. The idiot was barely doing twenty, even though the speed limit here was forty-five. Yes, it was raining, but not *that* hard. It was—she glanced at the dashboard clock—six thirty-seven. She was supposed to meet Carl at the restaurant at six thirty.

She slapped her palm on the steering wheel and swore. The windshield wipers arced back and forth, back and forth, moving at their highest setting, but even so water rippled across the glass as if the wipers weren't even there. The car ahead of her (the slowpoke!) was little more than a blurry outline with a pair of reddish smears for brake lights.

She looked at the clock again. Six thirty-eight.

Carl would wait, of *course* he would, and he wouldn't be upset. Being exactly on time was one of her things, not his. But that didn't make being late any easier to deal with, especially not after everything that had happened today. After her encounter with the little woman on the bicycle and the resulting panic attack, Tina had tried to make the rest of her scheduled sales calls, but while she managed to fit them all in, her timing was off. She was hesitant, unsure, unfocused, and the doctors she saw—when she got to see any; a number of receptionists didn't send her back— were short with her, cutting her off in mid-spiel and asking her to leave her samples and go, they hated to be rude, but they were especially busy today, just swamped. Summer allergies, summer flu, check-ups before summer vacations. A shrug, an apologetic smile. *You know how it is.*

She knew, all right—knew she'd had her worst day on the job since she'd started with Pharm-Tech. She was furious with herself for letting that weird little woman get to her. She'd been no diamond today. Hell, she hadn't even been a cubic zirconium.

And to top it off, now she was late for dinner with Carl. Tonight was supposed to be special, the night they made final decisions on the wedding, everything from the invitations to the reception and the honeymoon. She had a notebook filled with ideas, samples, and brochures that she was eager to finally show him. Like a typical man, he'd been ducking the detail-work of the wedding, but she'd finally pinned him down on making some choices over dinner tonight. She could've just gone ahead and picked whatever she wanted—she knew exactly what her preferences were—but she was determined to get Carl's input. After all, it was *his* wedding too, right?

But she wasn't going to get his input if she didn't make it to the goddamned restaurant!

She took a hand off the steering wheel, intending to lay on the horn so that the driver ahead of her would either speed up or pull over to let her by, when she noticed the way the water undulated across her windshield. It didn't look like it was coming down in drops anymore. In fact, it almost looked as if she were driving *under*water.

She gripped the steering wheel more tightly, eased off the gas, and concentrated on taking slow, deep, even breaths as she continued driving toward the restaurant at a crawl.

And if, out of the corner of her eyes, she saw dark, streamlined shapes moving gracefully through the dimness beyond her car, she told herself it was just an illusion conjured by the rain, that's all.

Breathe in, two-three-four. Out, two, three, four ...

Cocooned in water, arms and legs thrashing as she sinks, unable to stop her descent. She's a damn good swimmer, but her training is no use to her now. Her body's dead weight, falling into darkness.

The water is murky-dim, but she can still make out objects floating around her: foil-encased sheets of pills, all different colors, shapes and sizes; decongestants, antihistamines, anti-inflammatories, antibiotics ... loose wedding invitations on creme-colored paper, tumbling slowly end over end. Come celebrate the wedding of Ms. Tina Gensen to Mr. Carl Lockhart on Date Yet to be Determined.

A fish emerges from the outer darkness and comes swimming toward her. Its head is larger than it should be, long, fine tendrils trailing behind as it swims. No, not tendrils, she realizes. Hair. Blonde hair.

The fish swims up to her face and matches her descent so they can remain eye to piscine eye. It opens its tiny pucker of a mouth, and even though they are underwater, its voice comes easily and clearly to Tina's ears.

"Control is a—"

Tina doesn't want to hear. She covers her ears with her hands and tries to scream, but there's no air left in her aching lungs.

"—fragile illusion."

Tina woke up, fists jammed tight against her ears. It took a moment before she realized where she was—her bedroom—and what had woken her—the ringing of the phone on the night stand.

She sat up and reached for the phone, but before she could pick it up, the answering machine clicked on. She listened to her own voice greet the caller and ask whoever it was to leave a message at the sound of the tone.

A pause, then. "Tina? If you're there, pick up." Another pause. "All right, you're probably mad at me for standing you up tonight, and I don't blame you. I just ... well, I was going to say I got tied up at work, but that's an excuse. The truth is I'm ... not entirely comfortable with getting married. I know it's a cliché, the man getting cold feet, but that's not it. At least, not all of it."

A third pause, this one so long that Tina thought Carl was going to hang up, but he didn't.

"It's just that you can be so ... I mean, you always want things to go a certain way, and I don't ... Ah, hell. Forget it. Blame it all on me if you want. The bottom line is I don't want to get married. Not right now." A fourth pause, not very long this time. "Not ever." *Click.*

Tina sat there, struggling not to cry. Finally, a single tear rolled from the corner of her left eye, slid down her check and onto her lips. She told herself it didn't taste like lake water.

It continued to rain on and off all night, and the parking lot was covered with puddles. Tina sat behind the wheel of her car, waiting. She'd been here since five a.m., telling herself over and over again: *We can make this work, we can make this work, I KNOW we can ...*

At eight forty-eight, Carl's certified pre-owned Lexus pulled into the lot. Tina got out of her car as he parked and hurried toward him, running shoes splashing through puddles. She reached him just as he was closing his door, and she called out "Carl!" She tried not to sound pathetic, upset and needy, but she couldn't help it.

He turned toward her, car remote in one hand, briefcase in the other, and whatever emotions she'd expected to see on his face— joy, anger, confusion, irritation, disgust—there was nothing. His expression was completely neutral, and that was far worse than anything he could have said or done to her.

She was suddenly aware of how she must look to him. Carl was a mortgage broker, and he was dressed for work in a gray suit and maroon tie, while she wore a faded green T-shirt and jeans that were frayed at the cuffs. She hadn't washed her hair since yesterday morning, and it was a matted tangle. She hadn't put on any make-up either, and her face looked pale and washed-out, her eyes bloodshot and puffy from lack of sleep. There were other people pulling into the lot, parking, getting out of their cars, walking toward the office building, looking at the two of them and no doubt wondering who she was and what she was doing here, confronting one of their professionally attired brethren looking like trash. But she didn't care what anyone else thought; all she cared about was making things right between them.

"Don't do this to me, Carl. Don't do this to *us*."

"Jesus, Tina. There is no *us*, okay? Not any more. I'm sorry, I really am, but that's the way it is." He started to step around her, but she grabbed his arm and stopped him.

"Don't walk away." She spoke through clenched teeth. "We're still talking."

Now anger did twist Carl's features and he pulled free of her grip. "No, we're finished. In every sense of the word." Then more gently, "Just let me go to work, okay?"

Tina became aware of a faint sound coming from somewhere behind her, a soft *squeeek-squeeek-squeeek* of wheels turning. She ignored it. "Not until you agree to try to fix things between us— and we *can* fix them, Carl, I *know* we can. It'll take some work, and some time, but in the end it'll be as good as before. Better, even!"

"This *is* the end, Tina. Accept it and move on." Carl gave her a last look that was a mixture of love and regret, resentment and pity, before walking toward the entrance of his office building.

Squeeek-squeeek-squeeek. Louder now. Closer.

"It's not over, Carl!" she shouted. She took a step forward until she was standing at the edge of a large puddle. "Do you hear me? It's NOT!"

Other people heading into work turned to look at her, but Carl wasn't one of them. He just kept going.

The *squeeeking* drew up behind her and then stopped.

"I'm not going to turn around," she said, almost smugly.

She heard a rustle of cloth, a soft grunt of effort, then shuffling footsteps. The little woman had gotten off her bike. She hobbled to Tina's side and they stood there, silent, watching as the last few men and women made their way into the building to begin their workday. Moments later the parking lot was empty except for the two of them.

"It's not an illusion," Tina said, still stubbornly refusing to look down at the little woman. "Control *is* possible; all you have to do is—"

"Work hard enough," the little woman finished for her in a mocking voice.

Infuriated, Tina turned to the woman, intending to ... to ... she wasn't sure what, but intending to do *something*. But when she saw the woman's face, she froze. She was more fishlike than before—eyes wide, black and empty; cheeks covered with a scattering of scales; tiny gill slits on each side of her neck, opening and closing as they struggled to extract oxygen from the unforgiving air. But there was something else, something familiar about the shape of her nose, eyebrows, forehead, cheekbones, chin ... Then Tina realized where she had seen those features before: on her mother's face—and in the mirror every morning.

The little woman's pucker of a mouth stretched open in a hideous parody of a smile, revealing twin rows of tiny sharp teeth. Then with a swift, sleek motion she dove headfirst into the puddle, sending up a splash of water that smelled like rotting algae and dead fish.

Tina watched until the ripples subsided and the surface of the puddle grew still once more.

Walk away, she told herself. *Just turn around, go get in your car, and go home.*

But she didn't. The puddle was just a puddle, not even an inch of rainwater over blacktop, and she was going to prove it.

She took a step forward.

Water around her, below her, above her ... dark, so dark ... but she's not scared this time. She's not a kid anymore, and she can swim, swim like a goddamned fish. She's in control.

She kicks toward the surface. Her wet clothes make swimming awkward, but she concentrates on remaining calm and strokes harder. Soon she's rising through the black water. Up, up, up ... and still there is no light, only darkness surrounding her on all sides. Her lungs begin to burn for air, but she ignores their need and keeps swimming.

A thought occurs to her then: what if there is no surface—just an endless ocean of Nothingness above her?

She dismisses the thought immediately. There's a surface because she says there is, and she will reach it. All she has to do is work hard enough.

She senses unseen shapes moving in the water around her, circling, keeping pace with her, but she pays them no attention, continues moving her arms and legs, continues rising toward where the surface is—where it has to be.

Rising ... rising ... rising ...

COMMENTS

In 2004 (or thereabout), horror writer J.N. Williamson was going to edit a new volume in the legendary anthology *Masques* series.

However, Jerry was in his seventies and not in the best of the health, so Gary A. Braunbeck stepped in to pinch hit. (Jerry would pass away in December of 2005.) Gary asked if I'd be willing to contribute a story to the anthology, as well as a story for a small chapbook of tales buyers of the book's special edition would get. Of course, I said hell yes! I'd read previous *Masques* volumes, and it was an honor to have the opportunity to write a story for the new one. Since, then I've been fortunate enough to have stories in other legendary anthology series such as *Borderlands*, *Thrillers*, and *Shivers*. To a writer who read, loved, and learned from these books over the years, publishing stories in them felt like a serious leveling up in my career each time it happened.

"Waters Dark and Deep" isn't my first water/drowning horror story. That would be "Blackwater Dreams," a YA story which appeared in *Bruce Coville's Book of Nightmares II* in 1997. (I was asked to visit an elementary school where the students read "Blackwater Dreams" and talk to them. We met in the library, and I was surprised to find it covered with drawings that students had done based on my story. During the Q&A, one of the students asked what my best moment as a writer was. My answer: "This one's pretty good.")

In 1973, I was nine years old. As I mentioned earlier in this book, this was when I first became truly aware of death. My Uncle Red died from a sudden heart attack. The story I remember was that he went to his doctor for a checkup, got a clean bill of health, went out to the waiting room, sat down while he waited his turn to pay his bill, and died. When I told my parents this years later, they said it didn't happen that way. Maybe I was already rearranging reality in order to make more dramatic stories. But I was wary of trusting doctors for a long time after Uncle Red died.

When I was very young, my family used to travel in the summer, and in 1973 my mother's depression hadn't gotten so bad to keep her from wanting to go on a trip. My dad hooked up the trailer to our station wagon, he and Mom packed me, my younger sister, and younger brother into the car, and set out for Rocky Fort State Park, Highland County, Ohio. We stayed there for several days, and since I was the older kid—I *was* nine, after all—my parents let me wander around the park by myself. As a parent myself, I find it unbelievable the way people used to let their kids go off by themselves and do whatever they wanted in the 60's and 70's. It's a wonder any of us survived.

I was bored one afternoon and wandering around the park, looking for something to do. I ran into a kid carrying some empty cans, and I asked him what he was doing. He said he was collecting them to recycle, and that he could get money for doing so. I'd never heard of recycling (it wasn't a common thing in 1973 like it is now), and when he asked if I'd like to go with him, I said sure. Eventually, we ended up at the park's lake. The one warning my parents gave me before I left was to stay away from the lake since I couldn't swim. I didn't want to tell my new companion this. I didn't want him to think I was a wimp or anything, so when he walked onto the dock, I followed him. We walked halfway down, and I was looking at the water—I'm Pisces; even though I can't swim I *love* the water—for some reason the kid pushed me in. The next few minutes are burned into my memory. Flailing in the water, sinking, lungs burning and heavy, the smell and taste of lake water, bobbing to the surface, then going back down. Once, twice … The kid grabbed my wrist as I was going down for the third time, and he pulled me back onto the dock. I coughed and sputtered, and while I felt as if I'd breathed in half of the lake, I recovered quickly enough. In movies and TV shows, people always said if you went down for a third time, you were dead. I don't know if this is strictly true, but I believed it back then, and I felt as if I had narrowly escaped dying. As we walked away from the lake—my clothes soaked—I knew my parents were going to be angry with me. The kid said, "I've never been a hero before," and I wanted to beat the hell out of him because he was the one who pushed me. But I knew it was my own damn fault for going to the lake when I shouldn't have, so I said nothing. I wish I could remember the kid's name. I'd look him up on social media and yell at him for shoving me into the water fifty years ago.

When I got back to the trailer, Mom and Dad were mad, but not as much as I thought they'd be. They expressed no relief that

I was alive, had no reaction to my nearly drowning. I later asked my mom what she and Dad would've done if I had died. She said, "We wouldn't go on any more vacations." We never spoke of it again. As the years have gone by, I realized (thanks to therapy) that my parents weren't in touch with their own emotions and so couldn't help their children process theirs. But when you're nine, it's a hell of a thing for your parents to act like your near death isn't a big deal.

As I typed *near death*, I remembered that I had a stereotypical near-death experience. I found myself floating above the lake, watching my body thrash in the water as the kid tried to grab hold of me. Was this real or was it a dream I had later on, one which I conflated with the actual event? Who knows?

Bits of my real life in the story:

- Instead of fearing I'd lose a camera in the water, I had just gotten glasses, and I was afraid I'd lost them.
- "It's a good life if you don't weaken" was something my grandmother used to say.
- My oldest nephew's girlfriend—now his wife—was a pharmaceutical rep for a while before she decided to go to law school.
- The woman on the scooter was real. I saw her in the hallway of a strip mall around the time I wrote the story. I only saw her from behind. I never saw her face. She's the smallest person I've ever seen, and it was likely my imagination, but no one else around us seemed to notice her.
- My ex's sister's name is Karen, so she's Aunt Karen to my daughters. I don't recall any particular reason for using her name for the aunt who's briefly mentioned in the story. As I think I said elsewhere in the book. I like to add small details drawn from my life to my stories. It gives me a stronger emotional connection as I write.
- Having a fish swim up to a woman's face was an image I saw in Dario Argento's *The Stendahl Syndrome*, and it stuck with me.

WHAT MIGHT I DO DIFFERENTLY TODAY?

I'd have to think long and hard about including the woman on the scooter in the story if I were to write it today. I added her because I saw her around the time I wrote "Waters Dark and Deep," and sometimes I'll toss current experiences into a story to see where it goes. You can be mystical about it and say the Universe was telling me to add her. Or you can say that, by using experiences I couldn't have planned, I'm more likely to produce a story that's more original than I otherwise might. (I tend to think one or the other, depending on my mood.)

But there's no escaping the fact that the way I incorporated the woman on the scooter would be ableist today. (It was ableist then too, of course, but I wasn't aware of it at the time.) I added her because it was a surreal experience for me. I was well used to people of smaller sizes by the time I wrote this story and thought nothing of it if I encountered any. I'd thought any prejudice I might have in this area was long gone. But what struck me about the woman was how small she was. She might've been 18 inches tall, but I remember her as smaller than that. And seeing her only from behind, surrounded by people who didn't seem to see her made the event feel dreamlike to me. It was this dreamlike feeling I wanted to capture. But the woman in the story is definitely presented as a grotesque, dark being, and readers today would definitely see that portrayal as ableist. I made her a fish person in order to more tightly tie her to the story's theme, but that could be perceived as dehumanizing her even further, making her into a literal monster. If I were to use the woman I saw as an inspiration for a new story that I wrote today, I might make her the main character and have ableism be the dark force. But then again, I can only imagine what that might be like for her, so I would be appropriating someone else's story. And I hope that if I saw her today, I wouldn't find her strange at all, would see her as just another person going about her day.

I still have a long way to go to recognize and deal with ableism in myself, but one experience I had has gone a long way toward helping me. My brother Eric (who's 52 now), had a stroke when he was twenty. My ex and I were living in another state at the time, but we rushed into town to be there with the family. My ex had to return to work, but I stayed for a week. My brother was conscious and could think straight (more or less) but he couldn't move the entire left side of his body. After a week, I went back home, and it was another month or so before I saw Eric again. When I walked onto the ward where he was staying, I saw a nurse pushing a man in a wheelchair toward me. It took me a second to realize that man was my brother. Once I did, it felt like the entire world tilted onto its side, and when it righted itself, what I saw was my brother sitting down, where before all I'd seen was a wheelchair with an anonymous person attached to it. Something rewired itself in my brain that day thirty years ago. Ever since then, I never see a visible disability first. I see a person, and then I notice they have one arm. Sometimes I don't see the disability at all until a few minutes after we've been interacting.

This experience happened before I saw the woman on the scooter, and while I noticed her size right away, I clearly remember thinking of her as a person, not as a scooter with a tiny woman attached to it. But just because my perception of disability had changed after my brother's stroke didn't mean my brain had completely rewired itself. Horror has such a long tradition of viewing any human who doesn't adhere to societal standards of normal (whatever they might be in any given era) in terms of their physicality, psychological makeup, sexuality, etc. as monstrous, and it's a tradition that writers need to constantly fight—or at least be aware of—in their own work. I suppose it's possible for someone to take the idea of ableism in fiction so far as to say no characters should ever be presented as inhuman in any way, and any "monsters" should not be humanoid in any way, shape, or form. Would that be taking things too far? You'll have to decide that with your own work. I try to be aware of it, and do my best to ensure any monsters I present—literal or metaphorical—aren't ableist on my part. I noticed that I described someone as fat again for no good reason. That's something else I'm careful to look out for these days.

I've mentioned how water themes show up in my work a lot, and often my almost drowning works itself into my stories as a specific experience the main character had. I love water, but I was eleven when *Jaws* first came out, and it was one of the rare times my dad took me to see a movie. Like a lot of people of the time, I was traumatized by the intense suspense, and I still have flashes of fear while watching a killer shark movie. (They're the only type of film that still scares me.) Water makes such a great metaphor for all of fears and uncertainties. Anything could be in the water—anything at all—and we can't see it. The surface is like a molecule-thin line separating our world from the Realm Beneath, and we pierce that barrier at our own peril, as I learned when I almost drowned.

Is it good to have a theme or specific event in your life that you return to time and again in your work? It depends, I suppose. It could help brand you, and you likely have strong feelings about the event/theme which can make a powerful engine for your stories. And while readers of one particular magazine might not realize you've written yet *another* story about almost drowning, eventually someone will catch on, especially when you put out a collection filled with such stories. These days, I avoid using my near-drowning stories, although I did draw on it for the opening scene of my novel *We Will Rise* because I'd never included it in a novel before. When I write a water-theme story now, I look for different ways to approach the theme.

And that's what the next story does. So turn the page and take a look. (After you check out the exercises first, though.)

EXERCISES

1. Look over your previous stories to see if there's a recurring theme or a specific event that you often include. If so, make a list of all the different ways you can think of to put fresh spins on this theme/event. Pick one item on the list that appeals to you and write a story based on it.

2. If you haven't identified such a theme/event, think back on your life. Are there any impactful events you experienced that changed the course of your life? They don't have to be

traumatic ones like nearly drowning. And if you have had traumatic experiences, you don't need to revisit them just for a writing experience if it would be too painful for you. Once you identify a theme/event that resonates with you, make notes about how you might be able to use it in a story. Consider different ways you could rework the theme/event to keep it from becoming repetitious. Pick one of your ideas and write a story.

SWIMMING LESSONS

Originally published on the Delirium Books website (2006)

The humidity was so thick, you could take a bite out of the air and chew. Scott sat on the hard plastic bleachers in the front row, close to the rec center's pool, trying to ignore the dull ache in his lower back and wishing he had a more comfortable place to sit. *Getting old*, he thought.

Kelsey was at the far end of the pool with the rest of her class, holding onto the edge of the pool for support as she bobbed up and down in unison with the other kids. Scott supposed there was some point to the exercise, but it looked like all they were doing was learning to play Marco Polo.

The pool was filled with children of varying ages, from toddlers to middle-schoolers. At seven, Kesley fell somewhere in between. The kids' parents filled the bleachers, sitting hunched over, probably feeling the same ache in their lower backs as Scott did, their faces covered with slick sheens of sweat. Some talked listlessly on cell phones, some stared at open books with expressions of mild disinterest, and others chatted without energy or enthusiasm. They all looked as tired as Scott felt.

He was here alone. Carley had to work this morning, even though it was a Saturday. She scheduled all their daughter's activities and chauffeured Lindsey to them, often alone—something of a sore point between them. One of many these days.

Scott wiped sweat from his forehead and watched his daughter swim. The kids in her class were now lying on their backs in the water, holding onto yellow foam boards and kicking their legs with froglike motions as they swam backward. He sighed, and the sound was echoed by the parents around him. Sweat was dripping off of them now as if it were the height of August instead of early March.

Scott wondered for perhaps the twentieth time that morning why Carley had felt it necessary to go into the office today. Sure, they had an ever-growing mountain of bills to pay, but things weren't *that* desperate. She'd gone in last Saturday, too. He wondered if she were having an affair, wondered if he really cared. He wished he were having an affair, wished he were having *something*.

He let out a deeper sigh this time, this one echoed just as deeply by the other bleacher-parents.

Lindsey laughed as she finally reached the other side of the pool, and her teacher praised her determination.

Scott wished he felt as carefree, that a simple word or two of praise could delight him so easily. Had it ever? he wondered. He couldn't remember.

Sweat ran down his chest and back, soaking his clothes. Rivulets trickled down his legs, past his ankles, began pooling around his shoes. The acrid smell of chlorine seared his nasal passages, and he told himself that it was the pool water he smelled, nothing else. More puddles formed at the feet of the other parents as chlorine-scented sweat ran down the bleachers in widening streams.

So many worries ... unsatisfying marriages, soul-grinding jobs, perpetual bills, noncommittal lovers, inadequacies both real and imagined, unfulfilled dreams, diminished expectations ...

Scott glanced at the thermometer mounted on the wall. 92 degrees. God, it was stifling in here! The pool water looked so cool, so calm, so inviting ...

So free.

He heard Lindy's laughter as he reached up to smear away more sweat. His fingers sank into the wet flesh of his forehead, but he felt no pain. As if the action broke the surface tension of his body, Scott's form shuddered and collapsed into water. He felt a surge of a half-remembered emotion that he thought might have been happiness as his liquid substance splashed his seat, flowed onto the floor, and slid toward the edge of the pool. He was joined by the others, and their watery substances merged, flowed into the pool, and together they lost themselves in joyous oblivion.

Their children continued to swim and splash, not noticing that the bleachers were empty, laughing as they slurped in water and spit great mouthfuls of their parents at each other.

COMMENTS

Told you this was a different kind of water story.

There's no drowning here. Well, I suppose there is, if you count people turning in water and flowing into a pool as drowning. I don't. Whenever I've written about my near-drowning, it focuses on one person. But this story focuses on a group of people. Two groups, actually—parents and children. And the pool is a safe place. There are swimming teachers, lifeguards, and the parents themselves. The kids are safe and the parents don't have to worry about them. The story's threat doesn't come from water. In fact, water can be seen as a comfort and a release. When I came up with the story idea, I wrote it very fast, but I still considered ways to make it different than the water stories I'd written before it. I can't claim that I consciously thought about the elements I listed earlier in the paragraph. I did consciously try to make water the environment for the story, but not, as I said, the threat. So finding ways to take an opposite approach to your common theme can be an effective technique to avoid repeating the same concept and story structure.

I wrote "Swimming Lessons" using a technique I sometimes employ, especially when I'm stuck and nothing else seems to work. I begin to freewrite about my immediate surroundings, searching for anything that might be strange, disturbing, or just out of the ordinary. I record my own thoughts about this place and what's happening in it, then I start to imagine what my thoughts and actions would be like once the strange element grows stronger and begins to affect the place and the people—including me. If a theme or deeper idea occurs to me as I write—or, as in this case, I was pondering it before I began writing—I incorporate it. Almost everything except the end is true. I used a fake name for myself, and while I'm fairly certain my ex wasn't having an affair at the time—and I know I wasn't—it was becoming clear that our marriage wasn't going to last much longer. The lesson was early on a Saturday morning, and all the adults present seemed exhausted. I certainly was. We were drinking coffee and struggling to stay awake, doing our best to pay attention to what our kids were doing in the water. Well, some of us were. Other parents checked out the moment their kid hit the water, and they were doing anything but watching the lesson. That didn't necessarily mean they were bad parents. Likely most of them just needed a break from being Mom or Dad, if only for a handful of minutes.

I was forty-two when I wrote this, and I was just beginning to experience middle-age malaise, so I drew on that for the story. I love being a parent. It's the most important job a human being can have, and it changed me in so many ways, some of which I'll probably never realize. I sometimes get irritated at couples who choose not to have children, but not because of their choice. I get irritated if they start telling me about what it's like to raise children when they've never done it. Would you take cooking advice from someone who's never made a meal? Would you take sex advice from a virgin? Around the time I wrote this, a younger couple lived next door. We were talking across the fence one day, and the wife (I can't recall her name after all this time) talked about how she and her husband spent time at a lake with a friend who brought their young child along during a boating excursion. "It just shows you don't have to change your life if you have kids," she said. I didn't answer, but inside I thought: *It does if you do it right.* I thought deeply about all the things I experienced and learned as I grew into becoming my girls' father, and one of those things was how children replace us, and how we're supposed to help them do that. Yes, I still had my teaching and writing—still had something of an individual life—but my focus was on my daughters. Intellectually, I knew I'd return to having a full life of my own once they were grown, but right then at that pool, it felt like my sole purpose in life was to make myself obsolete.

Plus, the kids' joy at being in the water was a huge contrast to the adults' weariness. I could remember being a kid and having tons of energy and enjoying whatever I was doing wherever I was at, living fully and completely in the moment. I missed that feeling, missed being a kid, and I doubted I was the only parent there experiencing these emotions. (As I said earlier in the book, I never learned to swim, but I made sure both of my daughters took swimming lessons as soon as they were old enough. It's my revenge against the damn lake that almost killed me.)

Since I imagined the adults wishing to be children again, I had them turn into water. It was really hot that Saturday morning at the pool, and everyone was sweating, so I used those details to transition into everyone collapsing into water and flowing into the pool. Of course, you can't go back to being a kid, so the parents joined with the water the kids were playing in. They become one with the water their kids were learning to navigate, just as these kids would one day grow up and navigate their own adulthood. In the end, the adults get what they really need: relief from their stress and depression. I didn't have these exact ideas in mind when I wrote, but I felt them instinctively and incorporated them. It was only in retrospect that I was able to put the theme/events of the story into words.

Why did the adults turn into water? Fuck if I know. Earlier in the book I said I'm not a fan of overexplaining stuff in short stories, and that's especially true in flash fiction.

Flash fiction seems to work best for me when it's more impressionistic, more like a poem in some ways. My stories are like *Twilight Zone* stories in the sense that shit happens because it does, and the stories are really about how people respond to what happens.

Delirium Books closed its doors some time ago, but back then, editor and publisher Shane Staley had been posting flash fiction on the company's website, and he asked me to contribute a piece. "Swimming Lessons" was the result. Since I was knowingly writing flash fiction when I composed the story, I can tell you the choices I made to keep this story as short as possible, while still trying to give it a sense of character and an emotional core.

Despite the presence of other parents, all the kids, their teachers, and the lifeguards, there's only one real character in the story, so I used him as my focus. Readers would experience everything through his viewpoint, and I'd stick close to it throughout, relating the events in realtime. The theme of the story is big, the events are small. Dad watches daughter during a swimming lesson. Dad thinks existentially for a bit. Dad and fellow parents melt into water and flow into the pool with their kids. The end. This isn't a story like "Daddy," where it starts close to the end of a larger story. The few moments that pass in "Swimming Lessons" are the entire story.

Some tips for writing flash fiction:

- Establish the setting quickly, in the title or first few sentences. Use as few words as possible. Don't over-describe.
- Have one, two, or three important characters, no more, unless you're writing about a group as one. In "Swimming Lessons," there are two characters: the dad and the parents he represents, his daughter and the kids she represents.
- Focus on a single incident.
- The flash in the story, aside from its brevity, refers to the climactic moment. In general, flash fiction—especially when it's extremely short—is all (or mostly) climax. The usual structure of beginning, middle, and end is often replaced with a single moment.
- There is conflict, but it can be verbal, physical, or mental, and it's resolved quickly, in only a few steps. (You're not writing an epic adventure here.)
- Small endings work best. Twist endings can work, as long as it's not a cliché ending such as *It was all a dream.* In terms of actual events, while a bizarre transformation occurs in "Swimming Lessons," it's presented as four small things: sweating, becoming water, flowing into the pool, children play in that water. The thematic implications of the ending are huge, but the events depicted on the page—while weird—are small.

WHAT MIGHT I DO DIFFERENTLY TODAY?

Since I'm nearly twenty years older now, my perspective would be very different on the events of the story. If I went to swimming lessons now, I'd only be able to watch other people's kids and watch those people watching (or not watching) their kids. I would probably remember taking my girls to swimming lessons, so maybe memory would play a role in the story. I'd likely come up with different imagery than people turning into water and flowing into the pool. Or maybe I'd have the older man feel like he's lost purpose since his kids are grown and moved away and neither of them want children of their own. Maybe he'd be the only one who would turn into water. It would be creepy (and not in a good way) for him to go into the pool with kids not his own, so maybe I'd have him leave and turn into water outside—chlorinated water—and flow down a grate.

EXERCISES

1. If you were able to identify an event/theme in the last set of exercises, choose one of the ideas on your list and use it as the basis for a piece of flash fiction.

2. Take an idea from one your previous stories (a story that's not already flash fiction) and try to pare it down to its core concept, conflict, emotion, and action. Now write the story. How did it turn out? Is the flash fiction version better than the original? If so, why? If not, why? If you don't normally write flash fiction, could you see yourself doing more after this exercise?

LONG WAY HOME

Originally published in *Thrillers II* (CD Publications 2007)

Lauren felt the first raindrop on the back of her left hand. Without thinking, she called out, "C'mon, Alex! Time to go!" Before she finished speaking, another drop landed on the back of her neck. On some level, she was already starting to become suspicious—the drops were warm, and they didn't feel right on her skin, were too thick, too globby—but none of that registered on her conscious mind, not yet. She was too concerned with getting her son to listen to her.

"Alex?"

He was on the spider climber with three other kids, all of them about the same age, all arms and legs and mussed hair and crackling energy. They circled the top of the climber, playing a game of tag, shouting and laughing.

Another drop, this one striking the back of her right wrist. She didn't look at it.

Lauren took her hands away from the paperback thriller she had been reading, allowed the book to flip shut. She left it laying on the surface of the wooden table where she had been sitting, a surface now speckled with tiny red dots that she almost but didn't quite take note of.

She stood up and began walking toward the climber, toward Alex and his playmates, none of whom he'd met before this afternoon. She forced herself to walk at a measured pace and did her best to ignore the fluttery, crawly feeling growing in the pit of her stomach.

He won't fall, he's too old to fall, and even if he did, the ground beneath him is covered with cedar chips to cushion the impact. He couldn't get hurt if he tried.

The thoughts didn't help; if anything, they only increased her nervousness. It had taken quite an effort for her to sit and read while Alex played with the other children. This was a large playground, with swings, climbers, balance beams, and a large wooden structure built to resemble a castle. It half-circled the play area with stairs to climb up and corridors to run along, tunnels to crawl through, and poles to slide down. There was no way to keep a close eye on your children here, not unless you followed on their heels as they played. Lauren knew, because they had come here before, and she had shadowed Alex every time, never more than a few feet away, never taking her eyes off him, making certain he was okay.

But on the way here today Alex had asked if she would sit at one of the tables near the play area instead. She'd almost asked why, but she didn't because she knew the answer. Alex was seven; he didn't need, didn't *want* Mommy hovering over him while he played. Especially not if he hoped to hook up with some other kids and maybe make a few new friends.

And so she'd agreed and sat and pretended to read James Patterson, glancing at her watch every five minutes and trying to ignore the whoops and shouts of the children as they played, telling herself they were just having fun, that no one had fallen and gotten hurt. She'd managed to leave Alex alone for almost forty-five minutes, but she couldn't take it any longer, and the rain—though little more than a sprinkle so far—had given her a pretext to call off the fun and take him home.

"C'mon, Alex, it's starting to rain." She was almost to the climber now, and she felt more drops (more *warm* drops, *sticky* drops) plap against her skin. She noticed none of the other parents—mostly moms, but there were a few dads as well—weren't coming to get their kids. They stood around in clumps of two and three, chatting, ignoring their children, probably glad not to have to worry about them for a while. Lauren envied those parents. She couldn't stop worrying, no matter what.

She reached the climber and had to resist the urge to reach up and grab Alex by the arm to get his attention. She knew he'd resent her doing so, especially in front of the other kids.

"It's time we were going, Alex."

He kept circling the climber, pursuing and being pursued in turn. But he acknowledged her approach with a sullen glance. "Aw, Mom, just a few more minutes. Please?"

It was a warm Sunday afternoon in early May, and Alex's red hair was sweaty at the ends, his normally fair skin flushed from his exertions. He needed to rest, needed a drink of water. He did *not* need to keep playing.

Lauren felt a warm drop strike her throat, and she reached up and ran her fingers over the puckered flesh of a scar that peeked out from beneath the collar of her blouse. It was an old habit, something she often did when she was nervous.

"You've played long enough. I have to get home and get dinner started, and you have some homework you need to finish up before tomorrow." She used her Mommy Means It voice, and added a frown to reinforce her words.

It worked. Alex groaned, but he leapt down from the climber and landed with a soft *thunk* on the cedar chips.

"I gotta go, guys."

This elicited a couple *Aww mans* and *No ways* from the other boys, but a second later they returned to their game of tag as if Alex didn't exist. He started walking toward Lauren, dragging his feet through the cedar chips, and she almost held out her hand to him the way she had when he was a toddler, but she restrained herself. He was a big boy now, she reminded herself. Too big to hold Mommy's hand in the park—especially in front of other kids.

Alex wore a white t-shirt with a picture of SpongeBob Squarepants on the front, khaki shorts, and running shoes. His shirt was dotted with dark spots which Lauren at first took to be daubs of mud, though the ground was dry—or at least it had been before it started to rain. But as she watched, another spot appeared, then another, and she realized they were caused by raindrops hitting her son. But why were they so dark?

Then a drop struck his cheek, just below his left eye, and she saw why they were so dark. It wasn't a drop of water; it was a drop of blood.

"Hold up for a second, sweetie." Her voice sounded too high and quavery, despite her efforts to remain calm. Alex stopped obediently in front of her, and she reached out to touch the drop on his cheek. But before her fingers could reach his flesh, another drop splattered against the back of her hand, and she brought it to her face. The substance was thick, colored a darkish red that was almost black, and it gave off a sour, coppery tang.

Blood.

Her stomach dropped and a cold shiver ran along the length of her spine. *Impossible,* she told herself, her rational mind rising to counter her burgeoning fear. Blood simply did *not* fall from the sky. It was probably just a trick of the light; the sky was starting to cloud over, the air taking on a purplish here-comes-a-storm tint. Dark enough to make water look like blood. Or maybe the rain had been discolored by some sort of pollutant. There were a number of factories on the edge of town, smoke-stacks pumping out white plumes of toxic chemical cocktails into the atmosphere.

Whatever the hell this dark rain was, Lauren knew that she wanted to get her son out of it as quickly as possible. So despite her earlier restraint, she grabbed Alex's hand and began dragging him toward the parking lot. He made a squawk of protest and tried to pull free of her grip, but he came and that was all that mattered right now. They passed the table where she'd been sitting, and she saw her book sitting there, but she didn't want to take the time to get it. Instinct told her that she needed to get her son out of this rain *now*, and to hell with James Patterson.

Lauren had on a white blouse and light blue shorts, and as she towed Alex across the grass, reddish-black drops spattered on her bare legs and arms, warm and sticky. A wave of revulsion washed through her, and she almost stopped to smear the gunk off her flesh, but she resisted. She could worry about cleaning the stuff off of her and Alex when they were both safe inside the van.

As they drew near their Ford Aerostar, Lauren fished the keys out of her shorts pocket and thumbed the remote. The van's locks snicked open, and she pulled Alex toward the side door.

"Mom, what *is* this stuff? It's all ookey!"

"Nevermind that right now. Let's just get inside."

The Aerostar was dotted red-black, almost as if it were bleeding from dozens of pinprick wounds. The handle of the side door was slick with the stuff, and Lauren had to force herself to touch it. The metal was slippery, but she was able to slide the door open without too much trouble.

Alex hopped inside without being told, and Lauren saw that his hair was matted in places, and rivulets of (not)blood ran down his face and neck. His arms and legs were slick with the awful stuff, and his clothes were covered with dark, wet spots. From the way his eyes widened as he stared at her, she knew she looked just as bad.

"It'll be okay, honey. Don't worry." The words were automatic, like the pre-recorded phrases programmed into a child's talking doll. She wasn't sure she believed them, but she was a mom, and those were the sorts of things moms said, even when they weren't sure they were true. *Especially* when.

She gave Alex what she hoped was a reassuring smile, then slid the side door shut with a solid *chunk*. She turned and headed around the front of the van, half-running, and her left foot struck a slick patch on the asphalt and nearly slid out from under her. She managed to keep herself from falling, but a jolt of fiery pain lanced through her thigh. A pulled muscle, nothing to be concerned about. She continued more slowly, limping toward the driver's side.

She glanced toward the playground and saw the other parents gathering their children and beginning to head for their cars. The sky was almost night-dark now, and the rain—if it could be called that—was beginning to come down more heavily. She lowered her head and squinted her eyes to keep the muck from getting in them, and kept her lips clamped shut to prevent any of it from getting in her mouth. Whatever the hell this shit was, she knew she didn't want any of it inside her.

She reached the driver's door, tried to open it, but her fingers slid off the slick handle once, twice. Finally, she wrapped her fingers in the fabric of her t-shirt and was able to get enough of a grip to open the door. She climbed inside and slammed the door shut behind her. The place on her shirt where she'd touched the door handle was a large red-wet smear.

She sat in the seat, breathing heavily, heart pounding in her ears. They'd made it.

The windshield was spattered with dark-red globs, but Lauren could still see the other parents struggling to reach the parking lot, trying not to slip on wet grass that was becoming slicker by the moment, keeping hold of their children's hands as best they could, given the thick, red substance that was rapidly coating all of their flesh like a second grisly skin.

Lauren felt a pang of guilt. She should get out of the car, go to them, try to help. But she squashed the feeling. Her first—her *only*—responsibility was to Alex.

She inserted the key into the ignition and started the engine. Without thinking, she activated the wipers. After all, it *was* raining, right? The blades moved across the windshield, rubber edges leaving behind viscous red smears.

"Fuck!" She hardly ever swore, and never in front of Alex, but she figured if ever there was a time to curse, this was it. What was happening was insane. Blood—and it *was* blood and not some imaginary industrial waste product, let's face it—didn't just fucking fall from the fucking sky. But it was.

She thumbed the button on the end of the windshield wiper arm and twin jets of blue washer fluid splashed onto the red muck. She kept her thumb on the button as the blades moved back and forth, back and forth, doing their best to clear the blood away. She managed to clean enough of the windshield to see the other parents had made progress toward their cars, but not much. She stopped the washer fluid and turned off the wipers. Better to wait until the windshield was too gunked-up to see again to use the blades.

"Mommy?" Alex's voice was soft, and sounded like that of a much younger child. "Is everything okay?"

His question made her heart ache, and she felt tears threatening. She knew he didn't really want an answer, certainly not a true one; he wanted her to reassure him, to tell him everything was all right, and if it wasn't, to make it that way. That's what mommys were supposed to do.

She turned around and gave her son what she hoped was a convincing simulation of a reassuring smile. "Don't worry, honey. We're going home now."

Alex worked to return her smile, but it didn't last long. His eyes were wide, his face—his poor, blood-streaked face—was pale, and she wondered if he were in danger of going into shock. Hell, she wondered if *she* was.

She turned back around, her fingers reaching up to trace the line of scar tissue on her neck, and she heard the distant, faint sounds of a dog growling. Heard her mother say, *I'm sorry, baby. I'm so sorry.*

Her scar began to throb, but she knew it was her imagination.

She glanced at the rearview mirror and caught Alex's gaze. "Time to go." She threw the van into reverse and, mindful of the slick asphalt beneath their tires, gently pressed the gas. The Aerostar began to back up and she had to resist the urge to jam the pedal to the floor. The last thing she needed right now was to get into a wreck. Out of the corner of her eye, she saw that some of the other parents had reached their vehicles, were frantically shoving their children inside, starting car engines. In moments, the parking lot would become a demolition derby of frightened parents, all desperate to get their kids the hell out of there. Lauren and Alex had a head start, though. All she had to do was keep cool and they'd be on the street in a matter of seconds.

She braked, put the van into forward gear, pressed the gas. *Easy does it,* she told herself. *Easy-peasy,* Alex might have said. It had become one of his favorite phrases of late, and she found it ringing in her mind now, echoing in Alex's delighted little boy voice.

Easy-peasy, easy-peasy, easy-peasy!

And that's when the bodies began to fall.

The rain was coming down hard enough now that the world seemed cloaked in crimson mist. The bodies were nothing but dark shapes at first, plummeting from the sky, striking grass and asphalt, bouncing once, twice before finally becoming still. Not many: a half dozen or so that Lauren could see through the blood sliding down her windshield. She sat and stared, van in gear, foot on the brake, as the nearest of the shapes shuddered and started to pull itself up.

Sweet Christ, what now?

"Mommy, it's a monster!"

Her first instinct was to tell Alex that there weren't any such things as monsters, but the words died in her throat as she watched the creature closest to them stagger to its feet not more than ten yards away. She hit the washer fluid and wipers again, cleared enough of a spot to get a decent look at the thing. Whatever the hell it was, it had been damaged by its fall—*fall from where?* part of her wondered; there was nothing above the park but empty sky. Empty, that is, before the red rain. Stick arms and legs, all (she did a quick count) nine of them, were broken in several places, and the lopsided head hung to one side as if the neck were broken too. Its chest had burst open, and glistening organs spilled forth: purplish loops that resembled intestines, large pink things that might have been lungs, and other tumorous hunks of meat that she couldn't identify. She couldn't classify the damned thing; it looked like a hybrid of insect and lizard, but that description was a poor approximation at best. It was like nothing she had ever seen before—outside of a nightmare, that is.

She supposed Alex had named it best: *monster*. No other word fit better.

Despite its hideous injuries, the creature lurched forward as best it could on its broken limbs, each step making its exposed organs jiggle and flop about. Laura had the impression that the thing's glistening black eyes were fixed on hers, and she knew it was coming toward them.

"Mommy, I want to go home now. I want to see Daddy!" Alex was seven, but he sounded more like two. Lauren didn't blame him, though; she knew exactly how he felt. But she had to keep it together, for both of them.

Throughout the park, other creatures, all broken and wounded, began to rise and walk, even as more continued to fall around them. If one of the things was too badly hurt from landing, it would pull or push itself forward with whatever functional limbs it still possessed.

"Momm-MEEE!"

Alex ended the word in a shriek that brought Lauren back to herself. She removed her foot from the brake, pressed the accelerator (still resisting the urge to jam down on the pedal, and *Jesus*, it was the hardest thing she'd ever done), and the Aerostar began rolling toward the street.

There was a loud *crunch!* and Lauren jerked forward in her seat. She heard Alex cry out, wanted to turn around and comfort him, but the van was beginning to slide sideways on the slick asphalt, and she needed to hold onto the steering wheel, keep them from slipping into the grass where they might get stuck.

The Aerostar came to rest at an angle to the park's entrance, blocking it. She put the van in park and was relieved to realize the engine was still running. Thank God Daniel had taken it in for a tune-up last month.

Alex was sobbing, breath hitching in his throat. Rain pattered on the roof, louder now; it was coming down harder.

She turned around, smiled gently. "It's okay, honey. Someone just bumped into us from behind. We're fine." As she said these words, she realized she was a fool for stopping. So what if someone had rear-ended them? This was hardly a time to worry about exchanging insurance information and wait for the police to arrive to fill out an accident report. No doubt about it; she was in shock.

Horns sounded behind them, parents desperate to leave the park, to get their children away from the awful broken things that had fallen from the blood-red sky. How many seconds before they began trying to drive around the van, or worse, ram their way through?

Lauren faced forward again and gripped the gear shift. She thought she'd be able to get the Aerostar onto the street without having to back up. The passenger-side tires might have to go over the curb, but they could manage it. She hoped.

Alex still sobbing, rain still pattering, and then a loud pounding on her window. Lauren jumped, almost didn't turn to look. But she did, half-expecting to see glistening black eyes set in a chitinous-scaly face staring at her. What she saw was almost as bad: a crimson mask of anger, eyes filled with fury, mouth open and yelling, white teeth dotted with blood.

Then she realized what she was looking at—a man covered by red rain, presumably the driver of the vehicle that had rear-ended her. Between Alex's sobbing, the rumble of the Aerostar's engine, and the drumming of the rain on the roof, she could barely make out what he was saying, but it sounded something like, "What the hell kind of driving was that, you dumbass bitch?"

Lauren almost burst into laughter. The belly of the sky had split open and was gushing blood on the world, expelling monstrous, twisted things in the process, and this guy was pissed about tapping bumpers. Maybe he was in shock, too. Had to be, else why would he be stupid enough to get out of his car with those creatures—

Claws reached over the top of Mr. Road Rage's head and black talons sank into the skin just above his eyes. The man screamed, and Lauren saw that the creature's fingers were long and multi-jointed, like a spider's legs. The thing jerked the man's head back, and Lauren expected the creature to rip it clean off the neck, but it didn't. Instead, another hand reached around with spider-leg fingers and pried open the man's mouth. Red rain poured down his throat as he struggled to break free of the demonic thing that held him, but the creature was too strong.

Alex's sobs degenerated into a high-pitched keening. Lauren was distantly aware of it, but she couldn't take her eyes off what was happening outside her window. Mr. Road Rage's skin was erupting in greenish-black patches, and his eyes were clouding over, becoming shiny black.

The rain he had swallowed was making him into one of *them*.

Lauren felt suddenly nauseated. The rain was on her, still wet and sticky, on *Alex*, for godsakes. Neither of them had swallowed any, but what if it could be absorbed through the skin? It might take a little longer to work that way, but in the end it still would—

Something smacked into the passenger-side window. She turned to a green-black palm pressed against the glass, multi-jointed fingers ending in black talons. Another one, and this one wanted to get in, to get at Lauren and Alex, make them *drink*.

"Fuck this shit," Lauren breathed. She put the van into drive and jammed her foot onto the gas, not caring if they slid on wet asphalt, not caring if they wrecked, not thinking about anything except the overwhelming need to get the hell of there right fucking now!

The Aerostar fishtailed, slid across grass, juddered as it went over the curb, and then they were in the street, Alex clapping, cheering, "Go, Mommy, go!" Lauren felt a little like cheering herself, but she kept her concentration focused on driving. Their house was only a couple miles from the park, but she knew the drive home was going to be a hell of a lot longer than the drive here. She turned on the wipers, activated the washer fluid, and eased her foot off the gas. *Easy-peasy*, she told herself, and drove forward at a blistering five miles an hour.

When Lauren was five, her mother took her into the backyard to play while she weeded the flower beds. Lauren's mother was the type of person who could only concentrate on one thing at a time, so while she was busily yanking grass from between azaleas, she didn't see her young daughter walk up to the chain link fence, open the gate, and go through.

To Lauren, it was a fine joke to play on her mommy—a game of hide-and-seek with a little adventure tossed in for good measure. She'd never gone through the gate by herself before, wasn't allowed to be in the front yard without a grown-up watching her. But the forbidden nature of what she was doing only made it all the more fun. She knew not to go *very* far of course, but she thought it would be okay if she walked down the driveway to the sidewalk, maybe sat there and looked around the neighborhood, see who was out playing, watch cars go by, or just listen to the birds singing and feel the breeze move gently across her skin.

But she never made it to the sidewalk. Halfway there, a neighbor's dog—a big white boxer with brown patches on its flanks—

came trotting toward her. Lauren had seen the doggy before, running around the neighbors' backyard, sometimes sitting on the porch with one of its owners nearby. But Lauren had always been in the company of an adult before, and the dog had never seemed to take any special notice of her. But not so today. Today no one was around: not the dog's owners, not her parents. It was just Lauren and the doggy. She wondered how it had gotten loose, wondered if maybe it was doing the same thing she was, having a little adventure and playing a joke on its owners in the process.

As it came toward her, she smiled and said, "Hi, doggy!"

The boxer picked up speed, started running toward her, growling low in its throat. Instinct welled up inside Lauren, and she screamed and turned to run. She'd only managed to take three steps before the dog was on her, sinking its teeth into her shoulder and shaking her like she was its favorite chew toy.

She screamed and screamed, tried to pull free, rolled over and hit the dog with her fists to make it let her go. But the animal held her down with its forelegs and bit her hands, teeth shredding flesh and grinding against bone. Blood gushed from the wounds, fell downward onto Lauren's face, got in her eyes and blinded her.

Lauren was distantly aware of her mother yelling something, but she couldn't make out the words, couldn't even tell where they were coming from, near or far. All she was aware of was fur and claws, fangs and a lolling tongue, rumbling growls and hot smelly breath.

Then she felt fire erupt on the left side of her neck, and a shriek tore free from her throat just as much that of an animal as any noise the dog had made. The burning pain was swiftly followed by in-rushing darkness, and Lauren had only a second to wonder if she was dying before she knew nothing more.

She awoke in the hospital—white sheets, uncomfortably stiff bed, tubes running out of her arms. Her mother, eyes and nose red, sodden tissue clutched in her hand, sitting next to the bed. Lauren was sore all over, but the left side of her neck hurt most of all. She tried to move her right hand, but the tubes restricted her motion, so she used her left hand to reach up and feel the bandage taped to her neck.

"I'm sorry, baby. I'm so sorry." Mother's voice was so soft she could barely hear it. "I tried ... I wanted ... I was so scared, all I could do was stand there ... If Mr. Dupree from next door hadn't come ..." Tears rolled down her cheeks and Mother brought the crumpled wet tissue to her face.

Lauren watched her mother cry for a few minutes, and as she realized what had happened, something hardened inside the girl. She had been in trouble, her mommy had come to help her, but then her mommy *hadn't* helped her. Her mommy had just stood there while the dog chewed her up. Just ... stood ... there.

Lauren didn't make a vow then, at least not consciously, but from that moment when she realized how truly weak her mother was, a grim determination began to grow inside her. If Lauren ever had children, she would do whatever it took to protect them, no matter what.

It seemed as if the entire world was covered with blood. Streets, sidewalks, buildings, trees ... everything dripped crimson. Lauren remembered something she'd learned in school, a mnemonic device to recall the color spectrum: Roy G. Biv. Red, orange, green, blue, indigo, violet. It looked as if the other colors had somehow been removed, and only the R remained.

And still the rain fell—and with it, the creatures.

They made driving even more difficult, as if the blood-slick roads weren't bad enough. The damn things lurched across yards, along sidewalks, through the streets ... They were so slow that Lauren normally wouldn't have had much trouble driving around them, but the slippery roadways made any maneuver other than driving in a straight line tricky. She nearly lost control of the van a number of times as she detoured around one of the broken-limbed gut-hangers. Worse, the damn things kept falling. Several landed right in front of their van, necessitating a last-minute course correction, and one had even struck their roof, causing a dent that came down almost to the top of Alex's head. Luckily, Lauren had managed to keep control of the vehicle, and she watched the creature roll off into the street in her sideview mirror. But she kept driving, no matter what, all the while mentally repeating to herself: *Easy-peasy, easy-peasy* ...

The blood and the creatures weren't the only hazards. The other drivers on the road were just as bad, if not worse. No one seemed to be paying any attention to traffic laws—they drove wherever they wanted, however they wanted. She'd witnessed a half dozen wrecks and drove past the aftermath of at least a half dozen more. So far, she'd managed to keep them from getting into an accident, though there'd been a couple near misses.

They'd been driving for a half hour, and she estimated they'd made it three quarters of the way home.

Alex still cried on and off, though his tears came silently now. She occasionally made comforting sounds, told him everything would be all right, that it wouldn't be much longer, not paying attention to her own words, letting them come out automatically. But as she drove and continued to comfort her son, one part of her mind watched the creatures, trying to learn what it could, to detect some pattern to this madness.

So far, she had come to these conclusions. One: wherever the blood rain was coming from, that's also where the creatures were coming from. Two: the fall to earth damaged the creatures, but not so much that they couldn't function, at least for a while. Three: the blood rain could transform humans into the creatures, and the creatures wanted to hasten this process. Since she'd witnessed one creature forcing the man at the park to drink the red rain, she'd seen variations on the same scene over and over.

Four: the farther she drove, the more unhurt creatures she saw—no broken limbs, no protruding organs. She took these to be transformed humans who, since they hadn't fallen from the sky, were not damaged. Five: after a time (and presumably "reproducing" by forcing people to drink red rain), the wounded creatures succumbed to their injuries and died. She'd seen hundreds of the dead creatures lying about, had even accidentally driven over a few. It reminded her somewhat of the way cicadas would leave behind the shells of the early stage— the one where they resembled giant fleas—as they changed into their winged incarnation.

Six: while the creatures that fell from the sky seemed interested only in transforming humans, the "new" creatures demonstrated a slightly wider range of behavior. She saw some that forced unchanged humans to drink sky-blood, but she saw others that dug talons and teeth into soft, pink flesh and began tearing it to shreds. Wherever she saw this happening, she ordered Alex to close his eyes and tried to ignore the canine growling that rumbled in her ears.

She drove for what seemed hours more before finally seeing a street sign through her blood-smeared windshield. The sign was splattered with red, but enough of the letters were visible for her to make it out: Stafford Avenue. Their street.

"We're almost home, honey." Absurdly, Lauren hit her right turn signal as she pulled onto Stafford. She actually began to feel somewhat cheered. She'd gotten Alex through chicken pox, a broken collar bone, and having his tonsils and adenoids removed. She was going to get him through this, too. Damned if she wasn't.

You're not dealing with a simple childhood disease here, a voice whispered in her mind. *This isn't something antibiotics, hugs, or encouraging words will fix. The whole goddamned world has gone bugfuck. You can't protect Alex … not this time.*

She did her best to ignore the voice and kept driving.

Her neighborhood had become an awful parody of wintertime, with blood-red replacing snow-white. Trees, lawns, driveways, and houses were covered in crimson, and more was falling all the time. Sky-blood gushed from rain gutters, streamed down both sides of the street toward sewer grates. She wondered how long it would be before the sewers backed up and small lakes of blood began to form. Would the rain keep coming until, like a hellish version of the biblical flood, it covered the entire world? Or would it cease once some critical mass of infestation had occurred, when there were enough transformed humans to take over the job of turning the rest?

Most of the cars on Stafford Street were parked in driveways or along the curb, but there were a couple wrecks—a Geo Metro wrapped around an oak tree in someone's front yard; an SUV overturned in the middle of the road, its windows shattered. In both cases, the vehicles were empty, their drivers nowhere to be seen. Transformed, or maybe killed. Either way, they were gone.

Front doors were shut and presumably locked tight, though a few stood open, barely hanging on their hinges. It was obvious what had happened in those cases: one of *them* had gotten in.

Daniel.

Ever since the rain had begun to fall, she'd been so focused on protecting Alex and getting him home that she hadn't thought much about her husband. Normally, she would have called him on her cell phone in an emergency, but it hadn't occurred to her. Maybe it was the shock of dealing with the nightmare the world had become, or maybe she needed her total concentration to get this far, but it was almost as if she'd completely forgotten Daniel.

She took her cell phone out of the glove compartment, turned it on, and pressed the number that automatically called their home phone. One ring ... two ... three ... four ... and the machine picked up.

Hi, you have reached the home of Daniel, Lauren, and Alex. We can't come to the phone right now, but please leave a message after the beep. Thank you for calling.

The promised beep came, and Lauren said her husband's name several times, but he didn't pick up.

She disconnected, but she left the phone on, just in case he should call.

Had Daniel been out puttering in the yard when the rain began to fall? Had he gotten in his Camry, intending to drive to the park and help them? She hadn't seen his car on the way home, but visibility had been so poor, she could have easily missed it.

Or had something else happened to him? Something bad?

She didn't want to think about that. *A few more minutes and you'll be home. Daniel will be there, worried sick, but happy to see you're both safe. The three of you will sit down to watch the news, and the reporters will explain not only what the fuck is going on, but what's being done to stop it. And just like that, everything will be okay, or at least on its way to becoming okay. Easy-peasy.*

She turned around, smiled at Alex—at pale, trembling, wild-eyed Alex.

"Almost there, sweetie. Just hold on another couple minutes." Her voice nearly broke on the last word, and she fought back tears. She couldn't afford to let them come, not yet.

Alex didn't acknowledge her, didn't even look in her direction. He just continued staring forward.

Lauren turned back around. *He'll be okay once he's home. I'll make* him *okay.* She pressed the washer-fluid button to clean off the windshield again, but nothing came out. She pressed the button several more times, each more violently than the last, but still nothing. She'd used up the fluid.

She took her foot off the gas, but she didn't press the brake, not yet. She tried the wipers by themselves, but they hadn't worked before on their own, and they didn't work now. There was no hope for it: she'd have to roll down her window and stick her head out to see. She'd probably be okay if she kept her mouth closed. She and Alex had gotten plenty of sky-blood on them at the park, but they hadn't changed. And while she would be leaving herself vulnerable to attack by one of the creatures, she'd only seen a handful prowling the neighborhood so far. She supposed one could always fall from the sky and crash down on her head—and wouldn't that be an absurdly Loony Tunes way to die?—but she decided to risk it.

She started to roll the window down, but then her head snapped forward and the seatbelt dug painfully into her chest. She sat for moment, confused, hands gripping the steering wheel white-knuckle tight before she realized the van had come to a stop. The engine sputtered once, twice, then died.

"No." She tried the ignition, but the engine refused to turn over.

You hit one of the cars parked on the street. You couldn't see through the windshield anymore, and you took too long trying to decide what to do about it. Now here you are, less than a block from your house, and you killed your van. Smooth move.

She turned to check on Alex. He sat still, lower lip trembling.

"Are we home yet, Mommy?" They were the first words he'd spoken in what seemed like hours.

"Almost, baby. Just a little more to go." *Don't cry. Whatever you do, don't start crying, because if you do, you'll never stop.*

She unbuckled her seatbelt, then reached into the back to do the same for Alex. She didn't even consider the possibility that they might stay in the van and wait for someone to come help them. Even if there were police officers or EMT's still alive— or still *human*—out there somewhere, there were hundreds of other people in town who needed help. It could take hours, hell, maybe *days* before anyone could get around to helping them. And how long would it be before one or more of the creatures came scuttling down the street, searching for humans to change ... or to kill?

They didn't have any choice. They had to walk in the rain.

"Alex, listen to me carefully. We're very close to our house, but our van is broken. If we want to get home, we're going to have to walk. We're going to have to go outside."

Alex's eyes grew even wider and he began shaking his head.

"No. They're out there, Mom."

She didn't need to ask who he meant by *They.* "We have to, sweetie. It'll only be for a few minutes. We'll be okay."

He looked at her then, his gaze clear. "Promise?"

How could she? How could she not?

She smiled. "Of course. Now you sit there and wait. I'm going to open my door and go outside, then I'll open your door. After that, we'll walk the rest of the way home together, all right?"

A flicker of a smile, a nod.

"One more thing, Alex. When we're outside, we'll need to keep our mouths shut tight. The rain ... it's bad, sweetie. It won't hurt us if we just get it on our skin, but we have to keep from swallowing it. Understand?"

Another nod, more definite this time.

"Good." She patted his blood-caked cheek. "Let's go."

She took a deep breath and prayed to whatever deity might still be listening (if any) that one of the creatures wasn't waiting outside. She opened the door, but the only thing she saw was rain. She didn't allow herself to feel relief; she knew their luck could change any moment.

She stepped into the rain. She'd forgotten how warm and sticky it was, and she shuddered with revulsion. She experienced a surge of panic: what if she were wrong about how the blood-rain was absorbed? What if it just took longer to change you if it got on your skin?

She froze, unable to lift her hand to the van's side-door handle. Then she heard her mother's voice, soft, ashamed.

I'm sorry, baby. I'm so sorry. I tried ... I wanted ... I was so scared, all I could do was stand there.

The scar on Lauren's neck throbbed with a dull ache, echoing pain over two decades old but never forgotten. She wrapped her hand in her t-shirt, got a grip on the bloody side-door handle, and slid the door open. She then held out a hand to her son, the fingers crimson-slick.

He hesitated, and she hoped she wouldn't have to say anything to encourage him, didn't want to risk opening her mouth, but she would if she had to. But it didn't come to that. Alex took her hand and allowed her to guide him out of the van and into the rain.

Holding her son tightly, Lauren began walking down the street toward their house, careful to detour around the scaly carapaces of those creatures that had dropped dead in the street, like salmon dying soon after spawning. And if she saw other dark shapes in the crimson haze of the falling rain, *moving* shapes, she told herself they were too far away to worry about, and she kept moving.

The front door of their Cape Cod was open. Only a crack, but a crack was more than enough. Worse, the porch—which should have been protected by the metal awning above them—was covered with bloody patches that looked far too much like footprints for Lauren's comfort. She looked closely at them, trying to determine if they'd been made by human feet or—

"What's wrong, Mommy?"

Lauren looked up from the footprints. "Try not to talk. Until the—" *blood* "—rain dries."

She tried to think, but her brain felt sluggish, as if it were on the brink of shutting down. She couldn't afford to let that happen, not yet, and she forced herself to concentrate. If Daniel had been outside working on the yard when the rain began to fall, he might've rushed inside (leaving crimson footprints on the porch), failing to close the door behind him. He wasn't normally one to forget a detail like that—he was a T-crosser and an I-dotter if ever there was one—but there was nothing normal about today, was there? Even Daniel might forget to close a door on a day like this.

And maybe those footprints were left by something else, something that got inside. Maybe Daniel's nothing more than a pile of shredded meat and splintered bone lying on the carpet. Or worse— maybe Daniel wasn't Daniel anymore. Maybe he was—

She stopped that particularly nasty train of thought before it could go any further. There was no sign the door had been forced. No scratch marks on the wood or the knob. It was just ... open.

"Mom?" His voice was higher-pitched; he was getting worried.

"Hush now. Let me think."

"Mom, there's something in the street. It's ... coming this way."

No time left to think. She pushed the door open and pulled Alex inside. She slammed the door shut behind them, engaged the deadbolt and latched the chain. She doubted the locks would keep one of those things out if it wanted in badly enough, but she still had to try. Maybe with the door closed, the things would ignore the house, keep searching for someone still out in the rain.

And how long will it be before they start going door to door, killing or changing whoever they find?

Another thought to ignore. She put a hand on Alex's shoulder and steered him away from the door and down the front hall.

"Mom, why is there blood on the floor?"

She looked down, saw bloody patches on the tile similar to those on the porch. "Your father probably tracked it in." *I hope.* "Try not to step in it." What a laugh; as if they were dripping the goddamned stuff everywhere.

As soon as she said the word *father*, a hopeful look came into Alex's eyes. "Daddy?" he called, then louder, edged with panic. "Dad-deeeee!"

Nothing.

She tried. "Daniel? Daniel, are you here?" She listened for a reply, but again, there was none.

Tears began to roll down Alex's cheeks, leaving flesh-colored trails on his bloody face.

"Shhhh. It's okay."

It's not okay, you lying bitch. The town's fucked, maybe the whole goddamned world for all you know. Don't tell him everything's going to be okay when you damn well know it isn't!

She continued steering Alex into the living room. The carpet was stained with more blood, a violation in the place where they watched TV, played video games, listened to CDs, read books. This, more than anywhere else in the house, was the place where she, Daniel, and Alex came together as a family. It was bad enough when the blood-rain and the monsters and the insanity they represented were out there, but for the madness to be in *here*, in their *home* ... it was almost more than she could bear.

She forced herself to look at the footprints, to try and detect a pattern in them, as if she were a hunter examining animal tracks in the snow. She couldn't tell a thing, though, other than whoever (or whatever) had made them had walked all over the carpet, as if determined to stain as much of it as possible, or perhaps simply mark its territory.

Alex shrugged off her hand and turned to look at her. "Where's Daddy?" Demanding now, his tone saying she better have a damn good answer.

"Once the rain began falling, maybe he got worried and decided to go to the park and get us." She knew this wasn't true; Daniel's Camry was still in the driveway. She hoped Alex had been too afraid of walking in the rain—and what else had been walking out there—to notice.

"You mean he's ... outside?"

Wrong thing to say. "Wherever he's at, he'll be home soon. Let's get ourselves cleaned up, and I bet your father will be home by the time we're finished."

Alex frowned, and for a horrible instant she feared he knew she was feeding him a line of pure and utter bullshit, and that he was finally going to call her on it. But in the end he just nodded, wearily this time, she thought.

She looked at the TV sitting in its place of honor on the entertainment center, screen black and empty except for two small curved reflections of mother and son. She was torn; they needed to get this damn gunk off before it infected them, but at the same time, she was desperate for some news—*any* news—that might explain why all this was happening and what was being done about it. She debated a second more, then walked over to the TV, adding her own bloody footprints to those already smearing the carpet, and pushed the ON button.

The screen flared to life, high-pitched electronic tone and white letters against a blue background: EMERGENCY BROADCAST SYSTEM. STAY TUNED FOR FURTHER DETAILS. She and Alex stood before the TV for a minute, then another, but despite the screen's promise, no further information was forthcoming. Lauren tried flipping to other channels, but the same message appeared on them all.

She decided to leave the TV on, just in case, though she had a sinking feeling that it would be some time, if ever, before anyone came on with an explanation. Worse yet, maybe there *was* no explanation. The blood-rain was falling and the demon-things were coming down with it and reproducing simply because they were. End of story.

End of the goddamned world, you mean.

Lauren had been getting quite good at pushing away thoughts in the short time since the crimson rain had begun to fall, and she had no trouble getting rid of this one either.

"C'mon, let's go get this stuff washed off."

They left the living room and walked through the dining room. They had to pass the kitchen entrance to reach the master bathroom where the shower was, and Lauren saw the kitchen floor was, like the rest of the house, covered with bloody footprints. She also saw that the back door was wide open.

"Stay here. I'm going to go shut the door."

Alex gripped her hand tight, obviously not wanting her to go. She smiled and gently but firmly pulled free and walked into the kitchen, stepping carefully to avoid slipping on blood-slick tile. But as she reached for the door knob, a dark shape lurched onto the back porch. It was covered with blood-rain, but patches of greenish-black hide were still visible. Glistening obsidian eyes, multi-jointed talons, nine limbs—arms, legs, and some which she couldn't put a name to—all unbroken. This creature hadn't fallen from the sky; it was a newborn.

It's Daniel, she thought. *Who else would it be? He's been waiting for us to come home.*

There was no way to tell if this thing had been her husband— no scraps of his clothing clung to the beast, and there was nothing recognizably human left in its eyes—but in the end, it didn't matter who the creature had once been, did it? It could've been Daniel, a neighbor, or a complete stranger. Whoever it had been, it was a monster now, and it was coming for them.

She turned away from the door, started back toward Alex, slipping and sliding on the slick floor. She grabbed the counters to steady herself and shouted, "Go to the basement? Now!"

For a moment, she thought Alex was going to freeze with terror, but he turned and ran to the basement door. He threw it opened and pounded down the stairs, from the sound of it taking them two and three and a time.

Lauren kept making her way across the kitchen floor, trying at once to hurry and go slow so she wouldn't slip and fall. She knew that if she lost her footing, it would be all over for her. And if anything happened to her, there wouldn't be anyone left to protect Alex.

She heard the creature enter the house behind her. Moist, raspy breathing; clawed feet plapping on blood-covered tile. She prayed it couldn't move any faster than she could on the wet floor, that its arms weren't long enough to reach out and snag her before she made it back to the dining room. Did she feel air move behind her, as if clawed fingers sliced downward, almost but not quite connecting with their prey? Maybe.

She reached the dining room and the traction its carpet offered. She ran for the basement doorway, made it through, and slammed the door shut behind her. She locked it, if you could call the tiny switch on the knob that she turned a lock. She wished there was a chain, a deadbolt, a fucking crossbar, for christsakes, but who had those things on the inside of a basement door? Who ever thought the day would come when you would need to barricade yourself inside because there was a monster in your kitchen?

Something heavy slammed into the door, and Lauren started, nearly losing her balance. She grabbed onto the hand railing and managed to keep her balance, if barely. Another slam, this time accompanied by the soft sound of wood beginning to splinter. She turned and saw the basement below was dark. It was a wonder Alex hadn't broken his neck going down the stairs so fast without being able to see. She debated whether to turn on the light or not. Would they be safer hiding in the dark, or would it be better to see in case she had to fight the creature?

In the end, she flipped the light switch on. If there was even a chance the light would help them, she had to take it.

Another slam, the sound of wood cracking louder this time.

She hurried down the stairs, keeping hold of the railing so she wouldn't fall. Alex waited at the foot of the stairs, shivering as if he were outside in the dead of winter.

Slam!

"Let's go into the laundry room." She took Alex's hand and led him through the finished part of the basement—pool table, mini bar, dart board on the wall—and through an open doorway into the unfinished part where the washer and dryer were, as well as Daniel's workbench. A pile of dirty clothes lay in a clump before the washer, and past the workbench were haphazard stacks of empty cardboard boxes saved from when they'd moved here almost five years ago. Keeping the boxes had seemed to make sense at the time, but now Lauren wondered what the hell they'd been thinking.

Wood splintered like a shotgun blast, and she knew the thing had broken through.

Lauren steered Alex to Daniel's workbench as she desperately tried to think of what to do next. Have the boy hide in the dryer? No, he was too big. Under the workbench? No, the thing would see him easily. She scanned the tools lying on the bench, hanging on corkboard hooks. Hammers, screwdrivers, saws ... could she use any of them to try to fight the creature off? She knew they could die; she'd seen plenty of their bodies during the drive home. But she also knew they were tough as hell: the original ones that fell from the sky had survived their horrible injuries long enough to reproduce. Even if she could hurt the monster thudding down the stairs, she doubted she could do enough damage to prevent it doing what it would to them.

And there was no way to know what that would be. It was a newborn, and sometimes newborn creatures changed humans, sometimes they killed them.

Alex was breathing rapidly, and she was afraid he might hyperventilate. She found herself looking around the basement for a bag that he could breathe into, and when she realized what she was doing, she almost laughed. What did it matter if he hyperventilated now?

She strained to hear over the sound of her son's breathing. She thought the creature was close to the bottom of the stairs.

In her mind, she heard the faint echoes of a dog barking, saw the apologetic, shame-filled eyes of her mother looking at her daughter lying in a hospital bed. And she understood then how her mother must have felt upon witnessing her young daughter being savaged by a dog. Seeing her girl's blood spraying in the air, hearing her shrill screams of pain. No matter how much you worried, how close an eye you kept on your children, there were some things in life you couldn't protect them from. In the end, all parents are helpless, and it was the realization of that horror which had frozen her mother into inaction that day twenty years ago, and it was this same realization that Lauren was faced with now.

She reached up and touched the scar on her neck, and her fingers came away coated with sticky blood. For an instant, she thought the old wound had reopened, but then she realized it wasn't *her* blood on her fingers: it was sky-blood.

The creature that might or might not have once been Daniel lurched into view on the other side of the doorway. It hesitated only a moment before starting toward them.

Lauren knew she had only seconds left, but thanks to the blood on her fingers, she also knew that she wasn't helpless. Not completely. She ran her hand through her wet hair, got as much blood as she could on her fingers. She looked down at Alex, smiled, said, "I love you, sweetie," and jammed her fingers into his mouth, pushed them back as far into his throat as she could.

The last sound she heard was the boy gagging; the last sight she saw were greenish-black patches erupting on his skin; the last thought she had was *He's safe now.* Then she felt talons grabbing her hair, yanking her away from Alex, but it didn't matter what happened to her anymore. She'd done what she had to do, what any good mother would've done given the circumstances.

She had prepared her child to make his way in the world. Not the world as she might wish it to be, but the world as it was. A world that, from now on, Alex would call home.

She tried to tell her son she was sorry, but she couldn't get the words out before the monster that might have once been her husband did as it pleased with her.

COMMENTS

Here's another parent/young-child story. It's been weird to go back over these stories and realize how rare it is for me to write such stories now. Both of my kids are in their twenties and are on their own. I still could write about parents and young children, but I tend to pull story inspiration from whatever's going on in my life at the moment, so I'm sure I'll never write as many stories of this kind as I did back then.

This story had several inspirations. Cemetery Dance Publications editor Robert Morrish asked me to contribute to the *Thrillers 2* anthology. Four authors were invited—Gemma Files, R. Patrick Gates, Caitlin R Kiernan, and me—and we were asked to provide 20,000 words of never-before-published fiction. I can't remember for certain, but "Long Way Home" may have already been written, but since it was novella-length I hadn't sent it out anywhere. The small-press back then wasn't like it is now, and there weren't as many markets for novellas. Then again, maybe

I wrote it specifically for *Thrillers 2*. At this point in my life, I'm lucky I remember writing the goddamned thing at all.

In my comments on "Broken Glass and Gasoline," I told you how I'd decided to start a story with the image of blood rain. "Long Way Home" is the result. I began when the main character's world changes—when the first small drop of blood hits her hand. The playground in the story is based on a real one my oldest daughter loved to visit when she was a toddler. She used to call it The Big Playground. I really like that phrase. Maybe someday I'll use it as a title for a new story. One day during winter, I was driving home from school during a blizzard. My college had shut down early because of the weather, and it was a real battle to get home. I decided to draw from that experience, but use blood and skyfalling demons instead of snow. The house that the mom and son return to was the same one I'd lived in when writing "Broken Glass and Gasoline." By the time I wrote this story, we might've moved to a different house. I wanted to write an apocalypse story that had nothing to do with zombies (or at least where the monsters didn't look like zombies, although they function the same way as fast zombies do for the most part, except for the falling-from-the-sky bit). I wanted to write a story that more or less happened in real time, one in which I stayed in the moment with my character from beginning to end. I hoped this would increase the story's suspense. (Plus, if you need to get more length into a story, action scenes are a great way to do it.) But most of all, I wanted to write a story based on a specific idea, that it's a parent's job to prepare their child for the world they are going to live in, whatever kind of world that is. This is another story where weird shit starts happening without explanation. Given how fast events occur in the story and how severe they were, I decided there would be no time for anyone to figure out the cause for this invasion of monsters, so my main character wouldn't know either. Besides, she was too damn busy the whole time to worry much about whys. She wanted to save her kid. Why did the demon-things fall from the sky? Because the rain was, so I had them do so too. I thought it added to the craziness, just as some of the creatures landing so hard that their bodies were broken or they died did. It all added up to the bizarre mystery of the story.

I really liked how beginning with a strong image and moving on from there worked out in "Long Way Home," and the technique has become another one of my writerly secret weapons. If a story isn't working for some reason, I ask myself what the end would be, then I make it the beginning of a new story—and so far, the new stories that result have always been successful.

WHAT MIGHT I DO DIFFERENTLY TODAY?

There were no advanced smart phones with all the apps we have today, including Internet connectivity. If I were to write the story today, I'd have the main character try to use her phone in various ways to help her. She might learn from social media that the same event was occurring across the world, but I wouldn't have her find any hints as to why. I'd want to keep the reason for the blood rain and the demon attacks a mystery for both my character and for readers. Otherwise, I don't think I'd do much different. I might be tempted to try to write more stories in this setting, maybe even write a novel using it, but I'm not sure the premise is strong enough to support any stories other than *We tried to survive but were killed/transformed within the first few minutes.*

EXERCISES

1. Write a story that takes place in realtime. Say, ten minutes. Or, if you prefer, do a shorter exercise in five minutes. Movie scripts are usually written so one page equals one minute of screen time, so aim for around ten pages of story. Stay in the moment. Avoid summarizing or skipping ahead. Don't use flashbacks. Once you're finished, reread your story and see what you think of it. Do you like it? Is it a fast-paced thrill ride? Or does it feel shallow and underdeveloped? If you've never written a novella or novel, this technique can be an effective one to help you write scenes and add more length to your story.

2. Begin a story with the same image I started with—a rain of blood—then take it in your own direction. If you like how the story turned out, submit it to an editor. You're not plagiarizing if you do this, but if you feel weird about it, you have my official permission to use the image of blood rain in your own work and to publish it.

SHARP AS NIGHT

Originally published in *My Bloody Valentine* (Great Jones Street 2017)

In the dark, I hear you scuttle across the wood floor. You move swiftly past me, air flowing over my naked skin, and the sensation gives me goosebumps.

You stop and so do I. Both of us motionless, both of us listening for the slightest sound. You for my breathing, me for the soft *click-click-click* of your legs. But I hold my breath, you remain absolutely still, and neither of us hear a thing.

I run my hands across my chest, brush my nipples with my fingertips and try to imagine the soft skin of my hands is cold, firm, and smooth—like you. The thought makes me stiffen, and my penis grows half erect. I could reach down and stroke myself, make it harden the rest of the way, but I don't. I'd rather leave it like this for a bit, halfway between soft and hard. Anticipation makes culmination that much sweeter.

The room is large, and as the only furniture is the bed pushed up against one of the walls, sound echoes here in ways that make it difficult for me to judge where you're at. I think you're five feet away at least, maybe ten, but you're much closer than I think, and I feel one of your chelicerae gently touch the back of my knee. The claw's contact is unexpected—I didn't hear you move at all—and I can't stop myself from jumping a little. Fear zings through me, bringing with it an adrenal rush, and it's all I can do to keep from running. But I force my feet to remain where they are, imagine that they're glued to the floor. This is how we play the game, and besides, if I run you might become too excited and chase me as if I were prey. And when you caught me—and you would, because in a real chase I could never hope to outrun you—you could get carried away. The last time that happened, it took me almost a month to heal, and we couldn't play the entire time. I don't want to go through that again. Yes, the pain was unpleasant, but the separation from you was so much worse.

You step toward me and press your pedipalps against my hips, your chitin cool and smooth as polished bone. You push firmly, trapping my testicles between my legs, squeezing them. It hurts a little, but it creates a warm tingling in my balls, and my cock instantly hardens all the way. You move a little closer, and you stroke my ass with your chelicerae, their hair-like protrusions ticking, and the sensation sends an electric jolt shooting from my prostate to the tip of my cock. My shaft begins bobbing up and down in time with my pulse, and I feel the head moisten with semen. I almost come right then, but I grit my teeth and picture myself lying in the hospital bed, bandaged and healing, but alone. The memory makes the urge to climax retreat. It doesn't go away entirely, but I think I've got myself under control again, which is all that matters. I don't want to come too early, for my sake as much as yours.

You continue stroking my backside with your chelicerae, and you move your right claw into position and gently, agonizingly slowly, you take my throbbing penis within it and begin squeezing, bringing the two sections of your pedipalp together, one millimeter at a time. I know that you could close your claw like a pair of scissors and sever my penis from my body as easily as if it were made of paper instead of meat. But this is part of my excitement, feeling your power and strength, knowing that I've surrendered to you. My cock swells, tightens, and I imagine it first reddening from the blood trapped within, then purpling like a deep dark bruise. You continue squeezing, your claw tightening with surgical precision, and I don't know if I can take much more of this before my control shatters and semen shoots out of me like water from a firehose. But then you release me, and the sudden absence of pressure is almost more than I can take.

I expect you to skitter off so we can continue playing tag, but instead you back up, fasten your claws around my waist, and lift me off the floor. You carry me then, legs clicking in a rapid beat as you swiftly take me to the bed. I smile because I know you're turned on too, so much so that you can't wait any longer.

When we reach the bed you leap onto it, still holding me, and roll onto your back, legs in the air. You put me down on top of you and release me. I can't see your claws—the room is absolutely pitch dark—but I know you relax them to the sides until they almost touch the floor, as you always do. I move into position and my cock slides through your aperture and deep into your genital chamber. It feels like coming home.

I start moving in and out, slowly at first, the segments of your mesosoma rippling beneath me. But soon we're moving faster, both of us unable to hold back any longer. I'm thrusting harder, faster, and you're undulating so rapidly I fear I might be thrown off, like a bronc-buster tossed out of the saddle. My breath is coming in ragged gasps and with it wordless grunts. *Uh-uh-uh-uh-uh* ... I hear a hissing sound, and I know you're rubbing your pedipalps against your front legs, something you do when you're nearing climax. There's something else you do as you get close to coming, and I picture it now. In my mind I see your tail curl upward and inward, bringing your telson toward me. I see a drop of venom welling from your aculeus, like a pearl of semen emerged from my cock earlier. Then I feel the pin-sharp tip of your stinger touch the skin between my shoulder blades, dimpling the skin. I feel a line of liquid trickle along my spine, and I can't hold back any longer. I explode within you, but even as I come, even as I feel you climax beneath me—your genital chamber pulsing so much like a human vagina—I don't feel the one sensation I was hoping to, the one I've been waiting so long for. My cock continues its last spasms, but I don't care anymore, and I roll off you, my penis already beginning to soften. As I flop onto the bed—the unbroken skin of my back hitting the sheet—I begin to cry.

You crawl on top of me, close me tightly within your eight legs and stroke my tear-stained cheeks with the tips of your claws.

Then you whisper to me in a voice that sounds like the hissing your claws made rubbing against your legs.

I'm sorry. I couldn't. You pause. *Maybe next time.*

But you won't. You love me too much—or maybe not enough.

In the dark, you hold me, and I weep.

COMMENTS

This story was written in response to a submission call for dark erotica. I tend not to include much sexual content in my short stories, although I do put some into my horror novels to varying degrees, depending on what the story calls for. I'm not sure why this is. It's not a conscious choice on my part. I do think it's more difficult to include detailed sex scenes in short fiction simply because there isn't much room in a short story for detail that doesn't advance character or plot. It's not that sex scenes can't further character and plot, but they're often written as if the sex is the only thing that matters in such scenes. In order for them to function well—especially in short stories—they need to be multilayered, with physical sensation, emotional response, character development, plot progression, and conflict fused, sometimes in the same sentence. That's not easy.

One of the baffling things I've seen over my career is that horror readers can be downright puritanical when it comes to sex scenes. Want to decapitate a character in grisly detail? Horror readers love it. Show characters having sex? Horror readers will hiss like a vampire being shown a crucifix and avert their eyes. Now I'm only talking about some horror readers, of course, but however large or small a percentage of the overall audience it is, it's been a consistent reaction that I've seen for decades. Now if an anthology's theme is sexual in nature, that's different. I suspect readers who are averse to mixing horror and sex stay away from those books. But if sex scenes appear in a horror novel and readers weren't expecting them, that's when some readers become very uncomfortable.

It makes sense. Sex is one of the most basic aspects of human existence, and despite the amount of sex-related media in our culture, we don't get a lot of guidance on how to navigate growing into sexual beings. Sex ed classes may tell us how to insert slot A into tab B, but they don't address the myriad emotions that can result from the act. In a perfect world, people would have well-adjusted and fulfilling sex lives, but in reality, sex can mix wonderful positives and horrible negatives. It can bond people and help them enjoy life more fully, or it can be used to dominate, degrade, or wound them in ways both physical and psychological. But because sex is so primal and so important in human lives, it can be an extremely effective element to explore in horror fiction (or any type of fiction, for that matter). And if someone is demisexual, asexual, or aromantic, coming to understand your orientation and how it impacts any relationships you might have still means that the issue of sex is an important one in your life too, especially in a society that seems to be obsessed with sex much of the time. So, sex is fertile (no pun intended) ground for horror fiction. And the fact it makes some readers uncomfortable is a bonus. Horror fiction should not be safe, remember?

Do you narrow your audience by including erotic material in your horror? Sure, whenever we make choices in our fiction, we narrow our audience. People who don't like horror won't read your horror. If you write a story about vampires, people who don't like vampires won't read it. But readers who like erotic elements in horror will be attracted to your story, so if you lose some readers, you'll gain more.

Earlier in this book, I talked about how most writers are invisible to the world at large, and that even our friends and family won't be aware of our work if we don't tell them about it. Because of this, we can write about whatever we want without fear of what people will think. Sure, there's a chance that someone you know will check out your stuff, but it happens a lot less often than you might think. But when it comes to writing about sex, especially if you do it often, if family, friends, and coworkers find out, they will rush to check out your work and may view you very differently after they read it. Our culture is still very centered on cishet males, so men writing about sex is viewed as a positive sign of virility. If women write about sex, it's often seen as unseemly at best and sluttish at worst, and some people may think you're advertising sexual availability and hit on you. A lot of people write sexual stories under pseudonyms for that reason. During the lockdown phase of Covid, I decided to try writing an erotic short story with a horror element. I read a number of horror erotica stories then wrote mine. I chose a female pseudonym since much of the erotica I saw on Amazon was written by women (or writers using a woman's name). I chose Brianna London. My wife created a cover for me, and I self-published it on Amazon. The first cover was rejected (it showed a bit of butt cleavage), so my wife changed it, and voila! I was now a self-published writer of erotica. The story's called "Blood and Desire," and it's about a woman who seeks out a vampire to have sex with. I wrote it because when I discuss self-publishing in my creative writing classes, we talk about how writers often gravitate toward genres that seem to do well when indie publishing, and erotica is one. I also hadn't self-published anything before, so I wanted to see how difficult or easy it was. (In the mechanical sense of getting a book produced and up on the site for sale, not in the sense of trying to actually market the book and make it a success. That's a hell of lot more work.) I used a pseudonym since the story is focused on sex in a way none of my other fiction is, and I didn't want my readers to check out the story and say, "What the hell is *this?*" So if you decide to give writing erotica a try, consider a pseudonym.

The inspiration for this story was a photorealistic picture I'd seen on social media once of a man having sex with a giant scorpion. The image obviously dealt with the danger inherent in sex (danger of letting your emotional guard down and allowing someone see who you really are, danger of disappointing them, danger of STD's, etc.). But it also spoke to how outsiders might view a couple that seems to make no sense to them, such as when one person is considered extremely attractive by stereotypical standards and another isn't, or one is highly educated and their partner isn't. The image also made me wonder how beings of two vastly different species might communicate in a sexual way.

Plus, a guy having sex with a giant deadly insect? That's got erotic horror story written all over it!

I decided to make "Sharp as Night" about the physical/emotional connection between the two characters, and to show that in a single encounter. That meant it would work best as a piece of flash fiction. Instead of having the story based on the Jaws of Sex trope, I decided to make the two willing partners and emotionally connected lovers as well. The sex needed to advance character and plot, and the viewpoint character needed a goal he was trying to achieve so there could be conflict. The normal expectation would be that a human would fear being stung by the scorpion, so I decided to make that his ultimate goal—to die by the sting of his lover as a kind of ultimate orgasm. And since the stinger would penetrate him, it would be a symbol of him opening all the way to his partner. But instead of making the scorpion a predator that can't wait to sting its partner, it loves the man too much to harm him, and the scorpion's restraint breaks the man's heart. Once again, just making the opposite choices from what readers might expect allowed me to create a different—and I hope effective—story.

The point of view I stumbled across for this one was odd. It's ostensibly a first-person narrative, but the narrator is addressing his lover—who is the *you* in the story—which makes the piece kind of a second-person narrative too. I thought this almost hybrid point of view would help focus the story on the relationship between the two and show that it's emotional as well as physical, and also show the man's need. Because the story was a piece of flash fiction about this encounter and the emotional need underlying it, I didn't bother naming the characters or giving them any kind of background. Instead, I focused on present action and allowed it to show readers who these characters are. Description is obviously vital when writing horror as well as erotica, but it's tricky to get it right. If the language is too much like a cheap porno movie, the story becomes laughable, and if it's too clinically detached, it reads like a scholarly treatise on sex. Plus, you need to be able to blend horror description with erotic description in a way that, hopefully, creates a perfect blend of the two so that neither element dominates. I hope that's what I did with "Sharp as Night."

WHAT MIGHT I DO DIFFERENTLY TODAY?

It's difficult to say. (I was going to write *hard to say*, but when you're discussing writing sex scenes, you have to be careful of making unintentional jokes.) While craft-wise, this story required some complex writing, the story itself is super simple. Man and scorpion have sex. Man wants sex to culminate in his getting stung and dying. Scorpion can't do it. Man is sad. There's not a lot to work with there, and like "Daddy," I think that expanding the story with scenes of how the man and scorpion met, how they started to communicate, how they became attracted to one another, how they started their sexual relationship would only dilute the power of the encounter depicted in "Sharp as Night." I might go through and tinker with some of the language and see if I could get the blend of horror and erotica descriptions to work better. A similar image was shared on social media around the same time I saw the man and scorpion one. This image was of a woman sitting on a couch—head back, eyes closed—while a giant tarantula performs oral sex on her. Maybe I could use that image too, and have the human couple be husband and wife who have an open marriage but only with giant insect partners. Maybe the tarantula and scorpion come into conflict with each other, or maybe they each decide to kill their partner's spouse so they can have them for themselves, resulting in conflict. Maybe in the end they all make peace and live together with a brood of human-spider and human-scorpion children—a horror version of a large happy family. I don't know. What would you do to expand the story?

EXERCISES

1. If you don't normally write about sex in your fiction, try to come up with an idea for an erotic horror story or scene. If you want to try basing your story on an image, you can

do a Google image search of *sex with a monster*. Be warned, though. Some of the images might be disturbing to some people. *Sex with a ghost* doesn't provide as many inspirational images, but there are some. Same for *horror sex*. You can also try *sex with a vampire, sex with a werewolf,* etc. Remember to give the scene/story an emotional core. Try to make it mean something beyond bodies interacting with other bodies.

2. Write a story/scene based on an image that isn't sexual but which will provide inspiration for a horror tale. Google image search for words like *horror, bizarre, surreal, strange, terror, sinister* can work well. Along with more specific searches like *spooky forest, scary children, abandoned hospital, creepy carnival,* etc. Select an image that sparks your imagination and start writing.

TIL DEATH

Originally appeared in *Don't Fear: The Apocalypse* (13Thirty Books 2017)
Reprinted in *Year's Best Hardcore Horror: Vol. 3* (Comet Press 2018)

Audrey pushed the shopping cart filled with metal odds and ends along the cracked sidewalk, her husband Edmund trailing behind her, struggling to keep up. Sweat beaded on her upper lip, despite the slight chill in the air. The temperature never varied in the World After, never grew colder, never grew warmer. But Audrey was seventy-three, and even though she worked every day and was in good shape for her age, pushing a full cart took it out of her. She had no idea how long she'd been working. Time didn't operate the same way it had before the Masters' arrival. There was no day or night now. The sky was a perpetually hazy sour yellow like diseased phlegm with no sun or moon ever visible. Audrey didn't know if there even *was* a sun or moon anymore. For all she knew, the rest of the universe might've ceased to exist once the Masters came to Earth. Without day or night, Audrey had no sense of time. She could've gathered metal for five hours or fifty. There was no way to know. She only knew that she was tired all the way down to the bone.

The thrall mark on her forehead hurt like a fresh sunburn, and her head pounded with a rhythm that almost felt like language.

BRING, BRING ...

Maybe it was her Master's voice, maybe it was her imagination. It didn't matter. Either way, she had to make her delivery—so much depended on it. She stopped pushing the cart, released her grip on the handle, and turned around.

Edmund, her senior by eight years, was twenty paces behind her on the sidewalk. He was naked, his parchment-thin skin drawn close to his old bones. His limbs had been rearranged, so he could only move by crab-walking backward, and his head was turned 180 degrees so he could see where he was going. Not that his cataract-covered eyes could see much. His sparse body hair was wiry and snow-white, but his head was bald. Instead of a beard, thick worm-like growths grew out of his chin and cheeks. The fleshy tendrils were tipped with oozing pustules, and Audrey thought of them as pimple-snakes. They writhed with independent life, and Audrey couldn't look at them without nausea twisting her stomach. His mouth hung upon, jaw slack as if the muscles no longer functioned, and perpetual lines of drool ran from his mouth to moisten his pimple-snakes.

He didn't talk—or maybe he *couldn't*. Either way, Audrey was grateful. She had no idea how his mind functioned these days, but whatever distorted thoughts might spark and sputter inside what remained of his mind, she was glad he couldn't share them. He did make sounds from time to time: strange mournful hissings and tremulous bleats. His penis was always erect, so filled with blood it was purple-black, and a clear fluid that smelled like ammonia leaked from his ass. A line of the foul stuff trailed behind him on the sidewalk. In some ways, his body odor was the worst part. He stank like unwashed cock and balls that had been slathered in shit, and his breath was a sour-sweet reek that reminded her of rotting fruit.

Edmund hadn't always been like this, of course. Like so many things about the world, he'd changed since the advent of the Masters. So had she, just not outwardly.

It took him a while to close half the distance between them, but when he had, he stopped, gazed at her with eyes dull and lifeless as glass marbles, and lowered himself to the sidewalk. Audrey gritted her teeth in frustration. She *hated* it when he did this. She wanted to yell at him, shout that he should get his lazy ass moving, but she knew it wouldn't do any good. He understood so little these days. Not that he'd understood much in the last few years before he'd changed. She knew of only one way to get him going again, and while she was reluctant to do it, it was vital they made their delivery today ... before she lost her nerve.

She hesitated a moment, uncomfortable about leaving her shopping cart unattended. She'd worked hard to gather this much metal, and she didn't want to risk another thrall stealing it while she was trying to coax Edmund to get moving. Then again, the longer she remained in one place, the more she risked being noticed by another thrall. Or by one of the deadly creatures that roamed the World After.

Damned if you do, damned if you don't.

She once thought she'd understood that phrase, but she hadn't known shit.

She started walking toward Edmund.

In the first days after the Masters' advent, and the remaking of the world, Audrey had often thought it a blessing that Edmund's mind had been mostly devoured by dementia. He remembered her—more or less—but otherwise he wasn't aware of much. In a way, she envied him. She wished she was insulated from the World After with a comforting blanket of mental oblivion.

After the Arrival, she estimated they had remained in their home, doors locked and curtains drawn, for nine days before their supplies became dangerously low. Water was the biggest issue. Something still came out of the taps, but it was thick as tar, smelled like a mixture of cinnamon and turpentine, and had a corrosive effect on both metal and porcelain. She didn't want to know what it could do to flesh. Their only food was one nearly empty container of oatmeal and a few boxes of pasta. But she had no water or electricity to prepare any of it.

One evening—or perhaps morning, it was all the same now—she lay in bed, curtains closed so she wouldn't have to look at the phlegm-colored sky outside ... or at whatever hideous abomination might go lurching past. Edmund lay on the bed next to her, so motionless he might have been dead.

She couldn't remember the last time she had slept, was certain that she wouldn't drift off no matter how long she lay there, but sooner than she expected, her eyes closed and sleep took her.

She hadn't dreamed since the Masters' arrival, but she did so now. In the dream, she stood on a patch of bare earth enclosed by a high wooden fence with barbed wire all around the top. The white paint on the fence was old and peeling, the wood beneath gray and weathered. Mounds of scrap metal were piled at the corners of the fence, each taller than she was. In the middle of the enclosure was an open pit, ten feet in diameter, she estimated, maybe fifteen. The edges were smooth, almost as if the pit was a natural structure, though the perfect roundness of it argued against that. She stood several feet away from the pit, but she still had a good view of the inside. All she could see was darkness, so black, so deep, so *absolute*, that it seemed to actually be absorbing light, pulling it into itself and swallowing it.

Gazing into the pit caused unreasoning atavistic fear to well within her. She couldn't move, couldn't think, could only stand and watch, heart pounding rapidly in her chest like a small bird caught by a predator's mesmeric gaze.

She heard the Master's wordless voice for the first time then. It asked her a question, offered her payment for her service— unquestioning, unwavering. She spoke a single word in reply.

"Yes."

Fiery pain seared her forehead then, as if an invisible branding iron had been pressed to her flesh, and she screamed herself awake. Edmund woke too, confused and frightened. He began to shout and then to cry, and Audrey held him for a time, comforting him while her forehead pulsed with pain. When Edmund fell back to sleep, she took a flashlight from her nightstand, went into the master bathroom, looked into the mirror over the sink, shone the beam on her forehead, and saw her thrall mark for the first time. Along with the mark came knowledge: the location of the Master's lair and what was expected of her. The Master wanted her to get to work immediately, for it hungered. There was just one problem, one that she hadn't considered in her dream.

She fixed her gaze on the thrall mark's reflection, as if by addressing it she could communicate with her new Master. "I can't leave Edmund alone for long. He's not strong enough to work, and his mind ..." She trailed off, uncertain how best to explain it. But before she could speak again, she heard Edmund scream, a high-pitched shriek so intense it sounded as if he were tearing his throat to shreds.

She dropped the flashlight and ran back into the bedroom. Edmund writhed on the bed as his body reformed itself, bones breaking and resetting into new configurations. The transformation wasn't swift and it only became more painful as it continued, but when it was finished, Edmund had become a monstrously twisted thing, a creature strong enough to accompany Audrey while she worked. Her Master had done this somehow, she realized, in order to help her. It was, to the Master's alien mind, an act of kindness and generosity.

Audrey swallowed her rising gorge and forced herself to whisper, "Thank you," all the while unable to take her gaze off the horrible thing her husband had become.

The Masters came from elsewhere. Space, another dimension, a different time ... no one knew for certain. Some believed the Masters had ruled Earth in the distant past, perhaps even created it to be their plaything—or feeding ground—and long ago they'd left Earth for unknown reasons, but now had returned to reclaim what was theirs. They had no individual names—at least, none that humans were aware of—and no one had ever seen a Master. No one who'd ever lived to tell about it, anyway. Most believed they possessed no physical form, not as humans understood the concept. They lived in separate lairs and worked through thralls and monstrous servants of their own creation. Thralls were rewarded for their service with food, clean water, and electricity in their homes, and while wearing a thrall mark didn't protect you from every danger in the World After, it usually gave predators—both those human and those not—pause.

A thrall's main purpose was to feed his or her Master. Sometimes this meant capturing other humans and bringing them—kicking and screaming, if need be—to the Master's lair. But Masters didn't always feed on human flesh. From other thralls, Audrey had learned of Masters that fed on blood, human waste, and specific organs such as the pancreas. Some fed on inorganic objects such as used clothing, books, electronic devices, CDs, and DVDs. Some dined on more abstract fare: people's memories, emotions, or fantasies. All Audrey's Master required was metal. Any kind would do, although it was particularly fond of copper. Audrey had no idea exactly what happened to the metal after she threw it into the pit that served as her Master's lair, but she'd never heard it hit bottom.

Even though their Master gave them food and water—somehow made it materialize right in their home—Audrey was thin to the point of emaciation, as was Edmund. Masters might reward thralls for their service, but they were far from generous. They gave just enough for their servants to remain alive, and not a scrap more. And for this, thralls risked their lives day after day. But what else could they do? It was the only game in town.

In the World Before, Audrey's therapist had warned her about something called compassion fatigue.

It happens to long-term caregivers, she'd said. *Especially those whose loved ones suffer from conditions like dementia, which only worsen over time. You become emotionally exhausted, and—if you're not careful—that exhaustion can turn into feelings of resentment. Even hatred.*

That hadn't happened to Audrey. Not *before,* anyway. But now? Now it was hard to think of the loathsome thing that followed her around like some freakish dog as the man who had been her husband. She wanted to be free of Edmund as much, if not more, as she wanted him to be free of the nightmarish existence she'd inadvertently cursed him with.

The first time she'd tried to kill Edmund, she'd done it during a scavenging run, when she'd been picking through the ruins of a downtown office building. She didn't know what had caused the building's collapse. There was no sign of fire, no sign that something had struck the building. No wood rot, no crumbling concrete, no fatigued metal. It looked as if the pieces of the building had simply detached from one another and fallen into a jumbled heap. Edmund stayed away from the debris, guarding the shopping cart and watching as she walked through the odds and ends, searching for choice bits of metal. If anyone—or any-*thing*—came near, he'd let out a loud hissing sound. She had no idea if this was a conscious warning on his part or merely an instinctive reaction. Either way, his warnings came in handy.

As she searched among the debris, she came across large shards of glass, pieces of a window that had been broken in the building's collapse. A couple of shards were the right size to hold in one hand, and one of those was the basic size and shape of a butcher knife blade. She gazed at the glass knife for a long time before finally crouching down to pick it up. She gripped it like a knife, careful not to squeeze too hard so she wouldn't cut her hand. She was surprised by how heavy it felt, almost as if it were a real blade instead of merely a piece of broken glass. She gingerly touched the finger of her free hand to the pointed tip, then ran it along one of the shard's edges, again careful not to press too hard.

After a time, she stood, turned, and began making her way toward Edmund.

He watched her approach, no awareness showing in his milky eyes. His erection bounced several times, like he was a dog wagging its tail upon his master's return. He didn't react when she knelt next to his head. Didn't flinch when she touched the glass shard to his throat. Didn't do more than let out a soft hiss of air—was there a hint of surprise in that breath?—as she drew the shard across his neck, the sharp edge parting flesh and severing veins and arteries, bringing forth a gushing flood of crimson.

He turned to look at her then, blood dribbling past his lips onto his pimple-snakes. No expression, no recognition. And then he slumped to the ground and continued to bleed out.

She stood and stepped back to avoid the worst of the blood, but it was too late. It had spattered her clothes, slicked her hands ... so what did it matter if the widening pool on the ground touched her shoes?

She watched her husband die, surprised by how long it took for his erection to subside. But subside it did, and Edmund let out a last choked gurgle and stopped breathing.

Heart pounding, she stepped forward and pressed two trembling fingers to the side of his neck. No pulse.

She stood. She felt mostly relief, although there was some sorrow and guilt as well. She contemplated what to do with his body. He was little more than skin and bones, but he was still too heavy for her to lift. She couldn't get him in the cart, and even if she could, what would she do with him? There were no funeral homes anymore. She supposed she could bury him in their backyard, but something had happened to the grass. The edges of the blades were sharp as razors, and if you got too close they emitted high-pitched cries that sounded like tiny voices screaming. She wasn't sure it would be safe to try to dig there. Maybe if she just took his head ...

She heard the first predator then, approaching in the distance. A simian *hoot-hoot-hoot* accompanied by a leathery sliding, as of something large dragging itself across asphalt. The scent of Edmund's blood had drawn it, whatever it was, and she knew it wouldn't be the last. At least she wouldn't have to worry about what to do with Edmund's remains now.

She dropped the glass knife, took hold of the shopping cart's handle, and began pushing it away from her husband's corpse as fast as she could.

She didn't have any metal to deliver to her Master that day, and her reward for her failure was an excruciating headache brought on by her throbbing thrall mark. Even so, when she got home, she slept well for the first time since the Masters' arrival.

She woke to the sound of pounding at the front door. As she stumbled down the hallway, she already knew what she'd find waiting for her. She unlocked the door, opened it, and stood back as Edmund—who didn't have a mark anywhere on his body, including his throat—crab-walked inside. A thought drifted through her mind. *The cat came back ...*

She tried three more times. She used an iron poker to cave in Edmund's skull. She jammed a pair of socks down his throat to block his airway. Finally, in desperation, she took a screwdriver, rammed it through his left eye into his brain, stirred it around real good, and then did the same to the other eye.

He healed each time.

She had no idea if Edmund healed because of some quality his transformed body possessed or if her Master specifically healed him each time as a way to torment her. Whatever the reason, she knew she couldn't kill him by ordinary means. To end his travesty of a life, she would need *power*. The same kind that had transformed him in the first place.

She began to plan.

The skin on Audrey's right hand was raw and blistered. Pushing the cart hurt, but she couldn't manage it with only one hand, so she endured the pain. Edmund followed behind her on the sidewalk, moving a bit faster now, with a decided bounce in his step. She'd jacked him off, and it hadn't taken him long to come. It never did. But while what shot out of his quivering cock looked more or less like semen, it was an unhealthy gray, stank like sulfur, and was boiling hot. Getting Edmund off was a sure way to motivate him. He'd be in a good mood for hours—but she only did it when nothing else worked, for no matter how hard she tried, she always got some of his cock lava on her. Usually on her hand, but if his orgasm was particularly strong, he'd blast like a firehose, and there was no telling where she might get hit. Today, she'd been lucky. Only her right hand and a small spot on her left wrist had been burned. Painful, but nothing that would slow her down, and now Edmund was trotting behind her like an eager puppy, cock already swollen purple once more.

Audrey didn't look down as she walked. She knew better than to gaze at the cracks in the sidewalk. Something—or many somethings—lived inside and whispered the most awful things. If they caught you looking down, they'd whisper louder. They'd urge you to do things to yourself and to others, and the longer they whispered, the harder it was to resist them. Better to not set them off in the first place.

The town's population was sparser now. Many people died during the early days after the Masters' arrival, and many more had died since. Some had been sacrificed to Masters, some had been killed by the new monstrous predators that roamed the world, and some died at the hands of their fellow survivors, people who'd been driven mad or had turned savage during their struggle to stay alive.

Because of this, Audrey saw few people along the route to her Master's lair, and those she did see were sitting in alleys or on front stoops, heads down, sleeping or—just as likely—gone deep into their minds to try to escape the horrors of the World After. Every now and again one of them would look up as she passed, and she always made sure to turn her head toward them so they could see her thrall mark. That was usually enough to make them look away and lower their heads once more.

She was aware of other creatures, moving swift and silent between buildings, or crouching on rooftops and watching, motionless and hopeful. At times, she even had the sense that something was looking down at her from above, but when she looked up, she saw nothing in the sour-yellow sky. The land was filled with predators now—some large, some small, all deadly in their own ways. Her thrall mark would keep them at a distance, especially close to her Master's lair. She hoped.

Audrey never had cause to visit the Third Street Iron and Metal Company before the Masters' arrival. She didn't live particularly close to the place, either. She had no idea why the Master who laired there had offered to take her on as one of its thralls. Maybe it had broadcast a general call and she'd answered. Maybe she'd been chosen for a specific reason, one she'd likely never know. Whatever the truth was, she'd come to wish she'd never accepted the Master's offer. If she hadn't, she and Edmund would've been dead by now, probably from lack of fresh water, but that end would've been preferable to what their lives had become. Serving as a thrall was a mistake, one she intended to rectify now.

The word *company* seemed too grand for this place. A high white wooden fence surrounded the property, with the business' name painted in red letters on one of the outside walls. A section of a wall served as a sliding door which could be closed and locked, although it was always open when Audrey came here.

Since the only thing that could threaten a Master was another of its kind, there was no need for simple physical boundaries like doors and locks.

Audrey's thrall mark burned hot as fire. Her Master knew she was close, knew the *metal* was close, and it was losing what little patience it had. Audrey had heard about what happened to thralls that displeased their Masters. It made what had been done to Edmund look like little more than a mild swat on the hand.

She began pushing the cart once more, Edmund crab-walking obediently behind her.

The instant she set foot on the barren earth inside the fence, she felt the Master's power wash over her. She was officially in its lair now, the place where it was strongest. The air here seemed to ripple, like the distortion created by waves of heat rising off hot asphalt. Edmund made a small bleating sound when he entered. He was never comfortable in the Master's presence, but he always accompanied her inside anyway. She was counting on this—habit? loyalty?—now.

The ground was smooth, the path to the pit well worn, and the squeaking wheels of the shopping cart rolled easily over it. Normally, Audrey would push the cart up to the pit's edge—not *too* close—and then start lifting out pieces of metal one by one and tossing them in. If the Master was especially impatient and the cart's contents not too heavy, she might try to dump the entire load in at once. But she would do neither of these things today.

Her Master's impatience, its lust to feed, filled her, made her thrall mark feel as if white-hot coals had been slipped beneath her skin. She gritted her teeth against the pain, gripped the cart handle tighter, and started to run. She was seventy-three, malnourished and dehydrated, but fear, anger, and determination fueled her, and she ran with the strength and speed of a much younger woman. The cart's wheels squeaked so loudly they almost seemed to be screaming. The sound of the wheels combined with the sound of her heart pounding in her ears, and she couldn't hear if Edmund continued to follow her, if he too had picked up speed, his bare hands and feet *slap-slap-slapping* the earth as he fought to keep up with her. She hoped he was.

At first, she felt only her Master's all-consuming hunger, but then she detected a hint of puzzlement. Why was this thrall approaching the pit so fast? But before the Master could command her to stop, Audrey felt the front wheels of the heavily laden cart roll over the edge of the pit. She held tight to the handle as the cart tipped forward and fell into the darkness, pulling her with it. She looked back in time to see Edmund fling himself after her, and she smiled. The Master might prefer to eat metal, but she hoped it wouldn't mind an offering of flesh. *Two* offerings.

Audrey and Edmund tumbled down through black nothingness.

Audrey had no idea how long they fell. She'd lost her grip on the cart somewhere along the line, and she had no idea where it was. Edmund was close by, though. She might not have been able to see him, but she could still *smell* him. More, she sensed his presence the same way she'd sometimes wake in the night and know he was lying in bed next to her without having to reach over to confirm his presence.

The vertiginous feeling of falling had subsided around the time she'd lost contact with the cart, and she couldn't tell if she still continued descending. Without so much as a speck of light, she had no way of telling which way was up and which way was down, if such directions even meant anything in this dark limbo. For all she knew, she was hanging motionless in this void, and she might remain so until she died. Or worse, she'd stay like this forever, never dying, always awake and conscious. How long could a person exist like that before going completely insane?

She tried to speak but was unable to tell if her mouth produced any sound.

I'm so sorry, Edmund. I didn't know something like this would happen. I thought we'd die.

No reply from her husband. For once, she was glad his mind was gone. If they were trapped in this place, he wouldn't go mad. After all, he was already there.

After a time—how long was impossible to say—she sensed another presence, enormous and terrifying. It was as if she were floating in a sea and a silent ocean liner had drifted close without her being aware of it until the massive craft was almost on top of her. She knew she was now truly in her Master's presence.

She felt a wave of curiosity roll forth from the Master. It wasn't a word, wasn't even a human concept, but Audrey interpreted it as a single-word question.

WHY?

She didn't have to ask why *what*.

I couldn't let him go on living like he is. And I couldn't leave him.

She sensed only continuing curiosity, now tinged with confusion, coming from the Master.

He's my husband. We belong together.

The Master's confusion and curiosity vanished, followed by a sense of satisfaction, which Audrey interpreted as a single word.

UNDERSTOOD.

Pain exploded throughout her body as her bones, muscles, and organs began to shift and rearrange. She let forth a soundless scream, but she felt a hand clasp her shoulder—Edmund's hand— and she knew that, whatever horrible thing was happening to her, at least she wasn't alone. And then she felt Edmund's fingers join with her flesh, their skin flowing together like liquid putty, and if she could've produced sound in this non-place, she would've screamed louder.

Audrey and Edmund shuffled slowly into an abandoned building. The sign out front said the place once had been a night club called Spinners, but since neither of them could read anymore, the letters were only meaningless nonsense. They moved on four hands and four feet, two pairs of eyes scanning the debris inside the club for any metal. Poking out from beneath a splintered table, they saw a thin half circle of what looked like ... Could it be? *Copper!* Once, Audrey would've recognized this object as a bracelet, but now she only saw it as her Master's favorite delicacy. Audrey and Edmund were excited to retrieve the bracelet, but their combined anatomy made it difficult to move the pieces of broken wood. Yes, they had four hands, but their arms no longer bent the way they once did. Edmund carried a silver serving spoon they had found in a restaurant a couple blocks away, and he put it on the floor. The two of them then took hold of the table fragments with their teeth and slowly, painfully dragged them off the bracelet. When the object was fully revealed, Audrey leaned her head down to it. She used her thorn-covered tongue to lift it into her mouth, and then she gently gripped it between her serrated teeth. Audrey and Edmund couldn't operate a shopping cart, and so they were limited in what they could gather for their Master, but hopefully their meager offering would still be pleasing. Their Master would understand. After all, hadn't the Master made them this way?

Edmund retrieved his spoon, and they left the bar. Because of the tangled arrangement of their limbs, they scuttled and lurched instead of crab-walked, and they were more awkward than either of them had been on their own. But they'd learn to make due. Everything would be all right, just as long as they had each other. Once outside, they turned left and headed in the direction of the Third Street Metal and Iron Company.

Together.

COMMENTS

One of the things I like to do with my horror fiction is give it a twisted version of a happy ending, and that's what I tried to do here. Horror stories and novels typically end in one of two ways: the characters are completely and utterly screwed or they conquer the evil and survive (although not necessarily without scars). Since readers expect horror stories to end with one of these binary choices, I do my best to give them something else. As I keep saying, horror fiction shouldn't be safe, and that includes expectations for how it ends.

The only element drawn from my real life is the Master's lair. There's a scrap metal business just like it near the college where I teach, and I pass it every day on my way to work. As far as I know, no dark god lairs there. But then again, I've never stopped to check ...

I originally created the World After for a novella called *The Last Mile*. Whenever people write about Lovecraftian gods taking over the world, they portray it as the end for humanity. But one of humanity's greatest survival traits is that we can adapt to all kinds of environments. What if humans learned to adapt to the World After? I felt confident that some would. But what would those humans be forced to do, to *become*, in order to survive?

Another reason I created the World After was so I'd have a setting I could draw on for future stories. This is another of my writer secret weapons. If I'm invited to submit a story for an anthology and can't come up with any ideas, I consider falling back on one of the settings I've written about in the past. And if I want, I could use those settings as the basis for future novellas and novels. My zombie detective Matt Richter, from my *Nekropolis* series, lends himself to short stories well, and I've used elements from my first surreal horror/dark fantasy novel *The Harmony Society* in other stories. In a way, this technique is like doing tie-in fiction for your own work. I visited the World After in my story "Sorrow Road" for the anthology *Return of the Old Ones*. That story's about a mother and son stranded on a highway during the Advent, the moment when the Masters first appear on Earth.

Why didn't I go all out and use the Lovecraftian Mythos specifically? Because I wanted a setting that I could do whatever I wanted with, and I also wanted a setting that was free of all the baggage that the Lovecraftian Mythos has accrued since Lovecraft's death in 1937 at what seems to me now as the remarkably young age of 46. The less baggage, the stronger the core concepts, and since the World After is an apocalyptic setting, the simpler and more basic the ideas, the more they are in line with a simpler, more basic (and far more savage) world.

The World After is a hardcore horror setting. Maybe extreme horror, depending on how you define the two terms. Awful things happen there: horrible violence, twisted mutations, bizarre sex, along with lots of gushing bodily fluids, not all of them easily identifiable. I didn't intentionally set out to make a hardcore horror world. But given the circumstances—alien gods who transform the world into a nightmarish realm and people forced to do whatever they have to in order to survive and take care of their loved ones—

it seemed to me that extreme elements would naturally be part of the setting and the stories I told there. I love all varieties of horror, and as a creator, I think of them as colors of paint on my artist's palette. I use whatever color I feel I need to whenever I wish. Often my stories—especially longer works like novellas and novels—might have a scene of quiet, understated horror followed by a gut-churning scene of blood and guts flying everywhere. Part of this is conscious, another way of keeping readers off balance and making sure my horror isn't safe, but most if it is probably a result of the way I think. All kinds of thoughts and images swirl around in my head, changing from moment to moment, and when I write, that kind of chaos comes out onto the page. I think of this controlled chaos as one of the truer expressions of myself in my fiction, and it seems to have served me well enough so far. Not all readers like it, of course, but that's okay. I have my audience and I love each and every one of you. (But not in a creepy way!)

Sometimes readers and reviewers slot me into the extreme horror category, describing my fiction using words like *brutal*, *visceral*, *bleak*, *gory*, and *grisly*. I'm always a bit baffled when I see such comments, because to me the extreme elements are only one part of a story, and I don't go out of my way to include them or make them especially shocking. I wouldn't label any of my fiction extreme, but maybe that says more about me than it does how reviewers see my work! I've had three pieces (including "Til Death") published in volumes of *Year's Best Hardcore Horror*, and my novel *They Kill* was nominated for a Splatterpunk Award, so maybe readers and reviewers see something in my stories that I don't. Author Lawrence C. Connelly once told me that the world will decide how we'll be remembered, and I learned a long time ago not to argue with readers' opinions on my work. Besides, I love extreme horror. I just don't see myself as falling into the category. If I were smart and more market-driven, I might lean into the extreme more in my work or maybe try writing hardcore horror under a pseudonym to see how editors and readers respond. Maybe I will someday. But this illustrates a point. If readers and reviewers respond to aspects of your fiction that surprise you, consider exploring those aspects further. You might have strong talents in those areas that could result in your best, most popular work, and maybe take your career to a new level.

When I do write extreme horror, I approach it the same way I do any other type of fiction. I try to focus on character and base the story on an emotional core. In extreme horror movies, people—killers and victims alike—are usually ciphers, bereft of any real character development. That makes it easier for viewers to watch. They aren't emotionally invested in characters' fates, so they aren't emotionally affected when they die, no matter how horribly they go. Plus, movies only have so much time to develop characters and make them mean something to their audience. But in novels, you have a lot more room, and you can create more rounded, sympathetic characters, and readers will be devastated by what happens to them. The gold standard for this approach is probably Jack Ketchum's *The Girl Next Door*.

My advice for writing extreme scenes: make them vivid (especially in terms of sensory detail), stay in the moment, keep the focus on characters' reaction to what's happening, and give each scene an emotional core, even if it's only a small one. Try to make each scene specific to the viewpoint character in the scene. For example, if your masked killer attacks someone who has a phobia of death, maybe the victim will feel relief because now that death is here, they no longer need to obsess over it. The final question of every human life—How will I die?—has been answered for them. In general, less is more with extreme elements. If your story is wall-to-wall blood, guts, and disturbing sex throughout, all you'll do is numb readers—assuming they read to the end at all. The fewer extreme elements you use, the more they will impact the reader and stay with them.

When discussing writing erotica earlier, I said that friends and family may regard you differently if they read your work. The same applies to writing extreme horror, even if there's no sexual element involved. People without strong imaginations themselves don't understand how writers come up with ideas. They think everything we write is based on what we really think, feel, fantasize about, or have actually done because that's how *their* imaginations work. Be prepared for whatever reactions you may get, or consider writing your extreme work under a pseudonym, especially if you work with kids or teens in your day job. You don't need parents thinking you're a creeper.

A lot of the previous stories in this book were written when I was younger. I was in my fifties when I wrote "Til Death," so I focused on older characters. Yes, they're a couple decades older than I am, but I used my thoughts and feelings about aging as fuel for the story. I wonder how different the voice in this story is compared to the one in "Huntress"? Since I know the stories so well, I can't see the differences clearly, but maybe you can. No kids in this story, either. I decided mentioning any children (who presumably would be grown at this point) would only take away from the relationship between the wife and her husband.

WHAT MIGHT I DO DIFFERENTLY TODAY?

It's hard to say. I wrote this story only a few years ago, and I don't think I have enough distance from it yet to critique it properly. One thing I wanted to do was avoid depicting old age itself as part of the horror, and I hope I succeeded. Originally, I was going to make the Master in this story feed on something—or someone—alive. That's how I portrayed the Masters in *The Last Mile*. But if the Masters are symbols of chaos, why would they all be the same? To humans, there would be no rhyme or reason in what they feed on. Besides, by giving the Master a nonliving food source, I was able to keep the focus on the two main characters as protagonists/victims. (And if this Master lairs in a scrapyard, why wouldn't it eat scrap metal?) I might toy with the idea of giving the Master a more grisly appetite if I were to write the story today, but I think in the end, I'd leave it as it is.

During Covid lockdown, I wrote the first thirty pages for a new novella set in the World After, but then a tie-in project came up, and I abandoned that story. A couple months ago, I was looking at some of the stuff I wrote during lockdown but had never submitted anywhere. I liked those thirty pages, so I wrote a proposal for a novel based on them, and sent it to my agent. She's shopping it around, and if an editor bites, I'll write a larger story in the World After. Who knows? Maybe it'll become a series. One thing about writers: we always live in eternal hope, don't we?

EXERCISES

1. Go through your previous stories and see if there's a setting that you might be able to develop into a world that you could return to time and again in your fiction. Do you think the setting would work well at different lengths—flash fiction, short fiction, novella, and novel? If not, what sort of adjustments do you think you'd need to make in order for the setting to work at different lengths? Do you think the setting is rich enough for multiple stories to be told using it? If not, how could you make it richer?

2. If you don't normally write extreme horror, select a scene from one of your previously-written stories. If you'd rather, come up with a new scene. It can be something simple, such as a man out for a jog is attacked by a monster. Add hardcore horror details to the previously-written scene (or include them in the new one). Don't think of the details as extreme, disgusting, or repellent. They just are what they are. Don't rush through the scene, and try to focus on the victim's point of view. See them as human, not just as meat to be disposed of. Give them reactions to what happens to them that are specific to their character as much as you can. (Everyone will likely scream the moment a werewolf sinks its jaw into their flesh.) Once you've written the scene, ask a family member or friend to read it and tell you what they think. Assuming they don't think you're a serial killer now, ask them if there was too much detail or too little, and ask them about how you characterized your protagonist. How successful would you say the scene was? Can you see yourself writing more such scenes, at least sometimes? Why or why not?

3. If you already write extreme horror, choose a hardcore horror scene you have written or come up with a scenario for a new one. Try to rewrite/write the scene with as much restraint as possible. Often the threat of physical harm to a character is more impactful on readers than the harm itself. Minimal description of harm can allow readers to picture what happens in their minds, meaning that they provide the extreme details for themselves, thus making those details more psychologically effective. Once you finish the scene, give it to a friend or family member to read. When they're finished, ask them to describe what they pictured as they read and how they felt while reading. Were their reactions stronger than if the scene had been more explicit? Were their reactions milder than you expected? Do you consider the scene successful? Could you see yourself writing more scenes like this in the future? Why or why not?

HOW TO BE A HORROR WRITER

Originally published in *Vastarien* 2 (Grimscribe Press 2018)

If you want to be a horror writer, be washed from your mother's womb in a river of blood, kicking and screaming, writhing like an annoyed insect larva released from its egg. Feel rubber glove-covered hands clamp tight on a tiny arm and leg and pull you all the rest of the way free. Wail at the loss of the warm wet dark which is all you've ever known, scream in terror as harsh light stabs your eyes, shudder as cold air rakes your skin like a thousand claws of ice.

You look upon the face of the giant that holds you, its eyes all that's visible, other features concealed by cloth. There's another faceless giant present, and together they carry you to a small table and place you on a scratchy white cloth beneath a blazing miniature sun. You continue screaming as these horrible faceless creatures touch and probe you. You fight as best you can, but you're so small compared to them, so weak. They can do anything to you that they want, anything at all, and there's nothing you can do to stop them. They could tear the limbs from your body with ease, place a hand over your nose and mouth, sealing them shut. They could jam a thumb into your fontanel, sink the digit into your small brain and stir shit around in there. And when they finish, when they've had their fun, they could hurl you to the tiled floor to see how many times you bounce, maybe kick you back and forth like some sort of grisly toy. But the Faceless Ones do none of those things. They clean you off, take some measurements, wash you, and then one of the giants wraps you in a thin, soft blanket. You like the cloth. It's tight against your body, and you find this comforting. You grow quiet then, as much from weariness as from relief.

You're carried to a bed where a third giant lies. This one's face is bare, skin wan and coated with a sheen of sweat. You are held out to this new giant, and it reaches ungloved hands to you, lips pulling tight, ends curling upward. You find the expression as hideous as it is alien. The giant takes you and draws you close to its chest. The giant gazes at you with an expression you cannot read. Maybe it's happy to see you, maybe it wants to sink its teeth into your tender flesh. How can you know for certain what dark thoughts swim behind those large eyes?

The giant's lips part and sound emerges from its mouth.

"Hi, little one. I'm your mommy."

You have no idea what the sounds mean, but they feel familiar, or rather, the voice that speaks them does. You think you've heard it before, numerous times, but it was always softer before, muffled. Now it's loud and grating.

It comes to you then, less of a thought than an instinctive real-ization, something buried deep in your genetic code. This pale, sweaty thing holding you is your home. Only now you're looking at it from the outside. Until this instant, you had no concept of *inside* or *outside*, of being *a part* and being *apart*. This creature from which you emerged is large, yes, but when you were inside, the warm dark was the entire universe, and you were at the center of it. But now you begin to understand that existence is somehow both larger and smaller than the Warm Dark, and that not only aren't you the center of everything, you're so much smaller and weaker than everything around you.

You take a deep breath then, hold it for a moment, and then you let forth an ear-splitting shriek that, if it was a word, would be *No* repeated over and over.

If you want to be a horror writer, go to your Uncle Red's funeral when you're nine. He's not the first dead person you've seen. He's your great-uncle, and you have spent weekends at his house—along with your great aunt Becky and great grandmother

Alfretta—as long as you can remember. Uncle Red, Aunt Becky, and Great Grandma have always taken you with them when they do old-people stuff, like shopping at flea markets, visiting sick people in the hospital, or attending viewings of recently deceased friends and acquaintances. You have no idea how many viewings you've been to, maybe as many as a dozen, but while you found it awkward to be the only child present, the dead never bothered you. You knew they were dead in an abstract sense, but they all looked more like mannequins than people: skin waxy, eyes sunken, cheeks hollow, too much makeup on their faces.

But as Aunt Becky leads you up to the coffin, clutching your hand, her flesh thin as paper, bones underneath as light and fragile as a bird's, you know that this time is going to be different than those others. You're not afraid, and you don't feel nervous. Your stomach doesn't sink, there's no roaring in your ears, and you're not hit with a sudden wave of dizziness. You feel numb and disconnected, as if only part of you is present and the rest is somewhere else. As the two of you stand next to the coffin, your first thought—which you're too young to realize is a cliché—is that your uncle looks so natural, almost as if he might sit up at any moment, open his eyes, give a huge grin and say, *Gotcha!* Everyone would gasp and then burst into laughter accompanied by tears of joy and relief. But he doesn't move, of course. In fact, his body possesses a profound stillness that disturbs you on a primal level. The living are never so still, not even when sleeping. There's always some movement or sound, however slight. But there's nothing inside your uncle, aside from chemicals designed to slow his body's decay, and it's this Great Nothingness which disturbs you on a level so deep you cannot consciously touch it, let alone name it.

In the monster movies you love to watch on *Shock Theater*, hosted by Dr. Creep, death is embodied by some horrible creature emerging from the darkness, eyes wide with hunger, teeth bared, claws outstretched. In the movies, death is both awful and awesome, in the original sense of those words. It is, in its dark way, majestic and special. A monstrous beast, a servant of ultimate darkness, comes for you—*especially* for you—because you are the *victim*, and without victims, there can be no monsters. But there's nothing special about what's happened to Uncle Red. What's happened to him is no more remarkable than someone flipping a light switch to the off position. An everyday event—common, mundane, and utterly banal.

In the weeks and months to come, you will become obsessed with the idea that Time robs us of our life one moment after another, that it steals whatever happiness we can find even as it gives it to us. This obsession grows worse after you almost drown in a lake while on vacation with your family that summer. You ask your mom and dad what they would've done if you'd died. *We probably wouldn't go on vacation ever again*, they answer. They don't take you to see a psychologist. Only crazy people need a psychologist. It takes a couple years, but eventually you make an uneasy peace with Time. Yes, it takes, but it also gives. It brings new experiences, growth and healing. None of those things would be possible without Time. This realization helps, and you're able to go on with your life, but you never smile as broadly as you did when you were a child, never laugh so easily.

If you want to be a horror writer, learn to live with depression. It's your heritage, after all. Your mother is an agoraphobe who sometimes goes days without speaking, and your father—the very definition of an enabler—does little to help her. Only crazy people go to psychologists, remember? You don't know why she's like this. Your maternal grandmother, who you've always known as Nana, once told you that your mother was married before she met your father, and that her first husband abused her, although Nana didn't elaborate on the nature of this abuse, leaving your imagination to fill in the details for you. You wonder if whatever that man did to her made her like this. Years later, you'll decide her depression—like yours—is primarily biochemical, but for now you live with her stillness and silence, and while she's not as still or silent as the dead, she might as well be.

If you want to be a horror writer, internalize your parents' warnings—often unspoken or given obliquely—that the world is a dangerous place, that it's safest to stay home, but if you do go out, always be careful, always keep watch. Your sister's high school boyfriend is killed when he flips his car over one night after they argue, and when your brother is twenty, he'll have a stroke that changes him forever. Your older relatives begin dying one by one, and you hear stories of kids you knew in school dying in accidents, or by their own hands or—once—because they are stationed in Beruit and happen to be sleeping in the barracks when a terrorist drives a truck filled with explosives into the building. You get married and develop testicular cancer when your first daughter is only a few months old, and you're terrified that you'll die before you have a chance to be a father to her. You survive, but you'll always know that your body can betray you at any moment, that it eventually will one way or another, thanks to your old friend Time.

Your mother dies at fifty-nine, when your daughter is two, and you won't cry at her funeral. People will think it's because you're being strong, but it's really because you're relieved that she's gone. It's like someone opened a window and let fresh air in. You think it's a profoundly sad thing when someone's death makes the world a better place, but there it is.

You have a second daughter. Nana ends her days in an "assisted living" facility, really an unassisted dying facility as far as you're concerned. It takes years for her to go, and by the end her mind is almost gone, and she'll think your teenage daughter is your wife.

So yeah, the world's a dangerous place. When has it ever been otherwise? But it's the only world you have.

If you want to be a horror writer, divorce your wife. It's not a spectacular break-up. No hurled epithets or objects. Just a slow withering as your wife finds more excuses to avoid spending time with you. You come to understand that she finds your need to be connected to her emotionally burdensome, and that she's never truly enjoyed your company. A therapist will ask you to describe your marriage, and you'll say it's like you're a rock on the shore of a cold ocean. The sky is always gray, and wind and rain constantly buffet you. You end up in a shitty one-bedroom apartment that you share with too many roaches. You see your daughters half of the week, and the other half you feel like a ghost haunting your own life. You watch too many true-crime shows on TV because after paying spousal and child support—not to mention the debt payments on the bankruptcy your ex forced you into—you don't have any money to go anywhere or do anything. You only keep the damn cable so the kids have something to watch when they're over. Your ex takes the kids to her mother's for Christmas, and you spend the holiday watching police solve crimes with the latest forensic technology while you eat a festive meal of a single poached egg on a slice of toast.

You don't drink much, and you don't start now. You fear if you start, you won't stop. You find yourself contemplating suicide, not *too* seriously, but the idea seems increasingly appealing. Periodically, you find yourself staring at your reflection in the bathroom mirror. You're not sure why. You also speak these words: *There is no point to your continued existence.* Your reflection doesn't disagree with you. A friend of yours refers to depression as the Black Dog, and you think that's as good a name as any. You start taking meds to hold your own Black Dog at bay, and while they help, the damned thing remains close by, patiently waiting for a chance to bound forward and sink its teeth into your throat.

After a while, you start dating again, not that you have the money for it, but you're sick of being alone, and you're afraid of what you might do if you remain on your own. You try online dating, but the women you're matched with are incompatible at best and downright psychotic at worst. Still, you keep trying.

A blond woman arranges to meet you on Valentine's Day at a bar in a town an hour-and-a-half from your shitty apartment. She has large breasts, and she refers to them constantly during your conversation, as if they're the most important thing about her. She downs one drink after another, and she eventually asks you back to her condo. You didn't date much before you married, and you're surprised by how many women ask you to go home with them, or go to your place, after only talking to you for a couple hours. Don't they know that the world is a dangerous place?

She continues drinking once you get to her home, slamming down so much alcohol that you don't see how she remains standing. It's winter and an ice storm is starting outside, and while you know you should start heading home before the roads get too bad, you can't bring yourself to leave. You're not especially attracted to this woman. She's physically beautiful, but her personality is repellent. But you can't stand the thought of going back to your empty excuse for a life, so you stay, and before long the two of you end up in her bedroom, naked. She displays the breasts she's so proud of, and then smacks her fists into their sides.

"I don't have any sensation in my tits," she says. "You can do anything to them, and I won't feel it. Weird, huh?"

You don't have a condom on you—you'd think by now you'd learn to bring some considering how many women are eager to hop into the sack on the first date—so you take care of her with your mouth and hands. She comes, and you're surprised she feels it, considering how much alcohol is in her system.

"Your turn," she says with a drowsy smile. And then she starts going down on you.

The woman doesn't just suck your dick. She suctions it as if she's an industrial vacuum. The pressure is constant and unrelenting, and you find nothing remotely sexual in the action. There's a kind of mechanical desperation in the woman's efforts, and while you've avoided drinking much tonight—you've got a long drive home, after all—you wish you were drunk now, because what she's doing doesn't feel good. It *hurts*. You wouldn't be surprised if she sucks your dick off and swallows it, like a constrictor devouring its prey. You are so repelled by what's happening, your dick goes soft, but the woman doesn't stop. If anything, she works more frantically to get you hard again. You're about to ask her to stop when you feel a strange sensation. It's kind of like you're about to orgasm, but how can you if your dick's soft? You do come then, quickly and perfunctorily. When you're finished, the woman raises her head from your crotch and gives you an accusing look.

"What the hell was *that*?" she demands.

"I don't know," you say truthfully.

She says it a couple more times, placing emphasis on a different word each time.

"What the hell *was* that? What the *hell* was that?"

You quickly get dressed and get the hell out of there. It's after two in the morning, and icy rain is coming down heavy, but you don't care. You get in your car—a beat-up Camry that you haven't been able to afford having serviced for over a year—and start driving. The roads are coated with ice so thick that it feels like your car skates across the surface. The highway's even worse, and you can barely see because the streaks of ice form a white wall in the glare of your headlights. You should drive more slowly, more cautiously, but you don't. You think that it wouldn't be so bad if you lost control of your car, spun out, and crashed. With any luck, you'd die, and your daughters would believe it was an accident, never guessing it was really suicide, or at least a surrender to the darkness inside you.

But you make it home in one piece a couple of hours later, and the disappointment you feel at still being alive is like a ten-ton weight crushing down on you.

There is no point to my continued existence, you think.

Your agoraphobic mother becomes a ghost who not only haunts a house, she *is* the house. The lake you almost drowned in as a child becomes a setting for many of your stories. Your Uncle Red's corpse—or more to the point, the Great Nothing it represents—becomes the dark force of entropy which lies at the center of your fiction. And entropy, of course, is just another name for your old foe Time. The rest of it—your cancer, the divorce, the guilt over failing your daughters, the women you couldn't connect with—they're all there in your words, sometimes obvious, usually not. Your life is a funhouse mirror, and you look upon the distortions in the glass, and you write.

If you want to be a horror writer, answer questions from people, like *Where do you get your ideas?* and *How can such a pleasant person write stuff so dark?* And the kicker: *When are you going to write something* real? *You know, something true and meaningful?*

You'll stand there, Black Dog growling at your side, the taste of lake water on your tongue, still and quiet as a corpse inside, and you'll smile.

COMMENTS

As you already know, this story is very different from the others in this book, not only in terms of style and content, but also in the way it came about.

I've served as a mentor in the HWA mentorship program for a number of years, and a while back I was working with an award-winning professional playwright who wanted to get better at writing short fiction. His stories were, as you would expect, very well written, but they were written from a playwright's perspective—what characters say and what they do as an audience watches them. (Screenwriters think like this too, only they think of images that an audience sees, how those images move, and how they transition from one image to the next.)

I realized I needed to better understand a fiction writer's mind as they wrote, so I could better communicate the perspective to my mentee. So I decided to write a new story and pay close attention to how my mind worked as I wrote it. I wanted to write a story where the viewpoint character was very much into his or her own thoughts, a very *internal* story, since I was seeking that level of understanding. I decided to make myself the viewpoint character since I was observing myself, and I chose my favorite secret writing weapon (second person) so I could write the story more easily. Plus, I hoped it would create a distancing effect allowing me to be an observer while I wrote. I'd long been contemplating writing a horror writer's version of Lorrie Moore's classic short story "How to Become a Writer." The story satirizes how-to-write articles, presenting a list of extremely specific things that could only apply to the narrator and could never be replicated by anyone else. Some critics think Moore depicts a narrator who's so obsessed with herself that she fails to pay attention to the world around her. I always took the story to mean that each writer's path is specific to them, to the pattern of their own life, and thus every writer creates his or her own path by living. Regardless of Moore's ultimate intention, I decided my story would be an exploration of how I became a horror writer and what that means to me.

So I wrote "How to be a Horror Writer."

When I was finished, I wrote an email to my mentee relating what I'd learned about the space my mind inhabited when I wrote the story, and he said it helped. Here's what I wrote him:

I think the best way to describe how I think of audience (and of genre elements) as I write—and a way that might work best for you too—is to use the comparisons of a stand-up comic, an actor, or (in my case) a teacher. Comics, actors, and teachers might have prepared material to go over, but good ones also read the room in real time and make adjustments to how they present their material as necessary. They might not suddenly improv new material, but they make different choices about how they deliver it.

As I write, I imagine being the viewpoint character in a given scene, and at the same time I also imagine readers as an audience, as if I'm at once an actor on stage and the audience watching that actor. Genre conventions are in my mind as well, as if I'm performing Shakespeare or a comedy, etc. I'm aware of the general effect I'm trying to elicit from the audience. As I write a scene, my focus regularly shifts between being actor and audience, and I adjust what I write based on how I imagine the audience might respond. It's a constant back and forth.

My mentee said this was a great help. I was happy to be of service, and I had no intention of doing anything else with "How to Be a Horror Writer." It had served the purpose it had been created for, and it was far too personal to share with anyone. Plus, its form was experimental—a metafictional meditation on horror writing that was both autobiographical and written like a how-to article—and I thought that would work against it with editors. But like most writers, I suspect, I couldn't allow a story to languish on my hard drive for long, so I started sending it out. I tried horror mags first, but no go. Then I tried literary mags, especially those who said they wanted experimental writing, but again, without success. I thought *Vastarien* from Grimscribe

Press would be a good market. The magazine is focused on Ligottian themes, and my weird story seemed like it would be perfect. But *Vastarien* was currently close to submissions. I've been writing and publishing a long time, though, and sometimes if I contact an editor, they're willing to take a look at a story of mine outside the official reading period. I contacted John Padgett, he agreed to see the story, and both he and Matt Cardin loved it. They published it, and the story was nominated for a Shirley Jackson Award that year. Not bad for a story I wrote only to help me address a mentee's concern.

A lot of you are probably wondering how much of the material in the story is true. How much is me and how much is fiction? The short answer is none of your damn business. The long answer is what does it matter? From reading this book, you can identify parts of the story that are true since I discussed them in previous story comments. I hope that when nonwriters read the story, they get a better sense of where horror writers get our ideas: from everything that's made us who we are. I hope writers read the story and reflect on their own paths that led to them loving and writing horror. Maybe they'll also identify some major events and themes in their lives that they can draw on for future stories. I didn't write it as autobiography or memoir. I didn't write it so people could get to know *me*. But of course, no matter what we write, we're always showing something of ourselves to the world, aren't we? And yes, I did mention earlier in the book that one of the great things about writing fiction is we can reveal as much truth about ourselves as we wish and lie and say it's all made up. But I'm not lying when I say some but not all of the material in "How to Be a Horror Writer" is true.

Honest.

I dug deep into myself for this story, but at the same time, it was easy to write. It's not like the material was invented. I just had to allow myself to be open in a way I never was before when I wrote. Easier to do when I had no intention of ever showing it to anyone at the time. And it's a story I couldn't have written as a younger man. I think writers' stories are always better when they contain some part of themselves, but I don't know if I would advise you to put so much of yourself into a single story. Not only might you not be comfortable sharing so much with the world, but you might feel you've spent a lot of material you could've parceled out in your fiction in bits and pieces over the course of your career.

On the other hand, there's nothing so powerful in fiction as truth, however it's presented.

One thing you might try is writing your own "How to Be a Horror Writer" story to get in touch with how you came to be where you are. It might give you a better sense of where you want to go next. Remember, you don't have to show it to anyone. But if you do want to publish it, change the title, at least a bit. Maybe "How I Became a Horror Writer by YOUR NAME HERE." That way, anyone reading this book could write and publish their own version of the story. Who knows? If enough people write them, maybe we'll have enough for an anthology one day.

WHAT MIGHT I DO DIFFERENTLY TODAY?

I have no idea. Like with "Til Death," I wrote this story recently enough that I don't have much psychological distance from it yet. Because I originally wrote it for reasons other than publication, I put a lot of personal material in it, far more than I might have otherwise. If I were to write this story today, with a goal of submitting it for publication somewhere, I don't think I'd be able to put so much of myself into it. One of the reasons we write fiction is so we can hide in our stories, revealing ourselves without revealing too much. Even if every single element in this story was made up, the way it's written would make some readers take it as confessional nonfiction. I honestly don't think I would've ever written a story like this under any other circumstances than the ones in place at the time. But that's okay. A story like this probably works better as a once-in-a-career piece, although it might be interesting to revisit this story in ten or twenty years and see what perspective I bring to it then. I guess we'll see, assuming I'm lucky enough to live that long. (There's that dark horror writer's perspective again!)

EXERCISES

1. Write your own "How to be" story using this approach: a second-person narrator enumerating specific—and irreproducible—steps one can take to become something. You don't need to be confessional in your story if you don't want to. In fact, it doesn't have to be about you all. If you need some ideas, try one of these: How to be a Vampire, How to be a Movie Slasher, How to be a Horror Movie Victim, How to be a Bad Horror Writer, How to be an Unfathomable Cosmic God of Darkness, How to be Blood Spatter on a Wall, How to be a Monster Under the Bed.

2. Write a horror story using a nonfiction form such as a resume, a newspaper article, a blog post, a Wikipedia entry, an interview article, a textbook chapter, a gossipy tell-all, or any other form you can think of.

AFTERWORD

I'm typing these words immediately after finishing writing this book, and I'm honestly not sure what I've created here. A memoir in stories? A highly personal writing guide? A self-indulgent trip down memory lane? A Frankensteinian monstrosity stitched together from mismatched parts? A strange portrait of a writer as both artist and teacher? It doesn't matter what I think of it, though. All that matters is whether you found it interesting, entertaining, and useful for your own writing. As for what the hell it is exactly, you can call it whatever you want. After all, it's your book now, not mine.

ACKNOWLEDGEMENTS

Thanks to Jennifer Barnes and John Edward Lawson at Raw Dog Screaming Press for their willingness to go to the well with me a third time. Thanks to all the different editors who first published these stories, whether in markets large or small, and thanks as well to all the other editors I've worked with throughout the years, not only because you all helped me bring my stories to the world, but because your feedback and guidance made me a better writer. Thanks to my wife Christine Avery, who patiently listened to me bitch and moan about how I was never going to be able to figure out a way to write this book. And thanks to my daughters Devon and Leigh, who still don't know how many stories of mine they've appeared in as different versions of themselves. And special thanks to my agent and indefatigable champion Cherry Weiner. If she hadn't forgotten I'd told her to toss out the original proposal for *Let Me Tell You a Story*, this book quite literally would never have been written.

ABOUT THE AUTHOR

Tim Waggoner writes original dark fantasy, horror, and media tie-ins. His first novel came out in 2001. Since then, he's published over fifty novels and seven collections of short stories, among them fiction based on *Supernatural, Grimm, The X-Files, Alien, Doctor Who, A Nightmare on Elm Street,* and *Transformers.* Novelizations include *Halloween Kills, Resident Evil: The Final Chapter,* and *Kingsman: The Golden Circle,* while his articles on writing have appeared in *Writer's Digest, The Writer,* and *The Writer's Chronicle.* Waggoner is the author of the acclaimed horror-writing guide *Writing in the Dark,* which won the Bram Stoker Award in 2021. He won another Stoker Award the same year in the Short Nonfiction category for the article "Speaking of Horror," and in 2017, he received the Stoker Award in Long Fiction for the novella *The Winter Box.* In addition, he's been a multiple finalist for the Shirley Jackson Award and the Scribe Award as well as a one-time finalist for the Splatterpunk Award. His fiction has received numerous Honorable Mentions in volumes of *Best Horror of the Year,* and he's had several stories selected for inclusion in volumes of *Year's Best Hardcore Horror.* Waggoner's work has been translated into Russian, Portuguese, Japanese, Spanish, French, Italian, German, Turkish, and Hungarian. He is a tenured professor at Sinclair College in Dayton, Ohio, where he teaches creative writing and composition.

Let Me Tell You A Story

www.ingramcontent.com/pod-product-compliance
Lightning Source LLC
Chambersburg PA
CBHW021358090426

42742CB00009B/911